A Son Is a Son Till He Gets a Wife

A Son Is a Son Till He Gets a Wife

How Toxic
Daughters-in-Law
Destroy Families

Anne Kathryn Killinger

A Son Is a Son Till He Gets a Wife: How Toxic Daughters-in-Law Destroy Families by Anne Kathryn Killinger

THE INTERMUNDIA PRESS, LLC

ISBN 978-1-887730-13-6

To order additional copies of this book, please contact

The Intermundia Press
www.intermundiapress.weebly.com

INTERMUNDIA
PRESS

TABLE OF CONTENTS

I KNOW THIS IS A CURIOUS TITLE, and people who have never experienced the rejection of a son at his wife's behest won't understand it.

But those who have been through the experience—whose sons have married and turned against them as if they were dirt after all the years of love and care the parents gave them—will rejoice at finding this book and knowing they aren't alone.

Actually the desertion of parents by married sons is not uncommon. Would that it were! Almost every psychologist or counselor with whom I have talked knows of several instances in which it has happened. They speak of the great sorrow and agitation of the parents, mother and father alike, who can't understand why a child has turned on them.

"They could probably understand," they say, "if they had done anything to provoke the rift and separation. But they all protest that they've done absolutely nothing, and that their sons' behavior has hit them right out of the blue. That's what's so hard about it—it's unwarranted and unjustifiable."

Parents I've talked with have gone through all the stages of grief associated with the death of a loved one—doubt, denial, bargaining, anger, and acceptance—except that acceptance, the final step, is almost impossible for most of them. They try. But even years after the initial breaking off they find it hard to write "closed" to the case. Their love for their sons during their childhoods won't give up on those hardened men who say they want nothing else to do with them. They keep thinking, "If only we were to do this, maybe things would change," or "If only we could talk to him and his wife again, they might treat us differently."

A few days ago I heard from a mother now in her fifties who has not seen her firstborn son for ten years. They never had a quarrel. She had been a model parent. She and her husband divorced because he was an alcoholic and was physically abusive to her and the son, and she was especially careful during the worst times of the marriage and after the divorce to try to keep the son happy and help him to continue loving his father. But when the son married, his wife didn't want him to have anything more to do with his mother, and he broke off the relationship, just like that, the way one would snap a branch off a tree.

The mother had been to a ball game. A family member came up to her during an intermission and said, "Did you see who my husband was talking to over there?"

"No," she said, "I wasn't paying attention."

"That was your son."

She couldn't believe it. She had seen the woman's husband talking to someone, but hadn't noticed who it was.

"It didn't even look like the son I remembered," she said.

"He's big and fat now, and doesn't have any hair."

The most painful part, she said—as if anything could be more painful than being rejected by a son she loved—was that she had never seen her granddaughter, who she heard had been born six years earlier.

She had another child, a daughter, and the daughter lived near her and shared her two small sons with her. But there was still a big hole in her heart for the granddaughter she had never seen.

Most parents' stories are similar. They enjoyed their sons during childhood and young adulthood. There were no serious problems. But when the sons married, everything changed. Suddenly the parents were regarded as "bad" persons who might interfere with the sons' relationships with their wives. The sons couldn't say why they were bad. They just didn't want any more to do with them. They had their own families now, and were writing *finis* to the old relationships.

Thank God, not all sons behave this way and not all daughters-in-law make their husbands stop seeing their parents. In fact, most sons and daughters-in-law are normal, friendly, respectful, and eager to please both sets of in-laws.

But there seem to be an increasing number of sons who, once they get married, decide that they want nothing else to do with their parents. My own estimate is that this is the case about ten percent of the time. Ten percent may not seem a very big rate. But it would be awfully big if we said one out of ten persons now will have lymphoma or one out of ten persons will die at the hand of an assassin. In those cases, even one out of twenty would be a horrible percentage.

Mickey Spillane, the inventor of the hard-boiled detective story, once said that he wrote the kind of books he wanted to read. I've written this book because I wanted to read one like it and couldn't find one.

I was surprised that no one had ever written anything about lost sons. But I think I know the reason. It's because most parents think their case is unique. In fact, many of them are ashamed to tell anyone that their sons won't see them or come to visit with the grandchildren because they think it makes them sound like monsters. The majority of their friends don't have this kind of problem, so they don't feel secure enough to announce that they do.

It's the same as with parents who have Downs syndrome children. Until a few years ago, many parents of Downs children quietly placed them in special homes without telling anybody. There is more openness about such things now because there has been more publicity about them. And in a few years there will be more openness about parents whose sons have forsworn them after getting married, because the evidence will show that parents are seldom responsible for this kind of behavior.

That's part of my mission in writing this book. I want to say to parents who see the title on a bookstore counter and quietly buy a copy to read in the privacy of their homes, "You don't need to be ashamed of the fact that your son treats you this way. It's a lot more common than you think. In fact, you yourselves probably know at least one or two couples whose son does this and they simply haven't told you about it, for the same reason that you haven't told them. There's nothing wrong with either of you, and you didn't do anything to cause what has happened."

There are a number of couples' stories in this book—people all the way from New York to California and Michigan to Louisiana. My husband and I have known all of them personally—or at least he has. He is a minister, and has pastored a lot of churches and counseled thousands of people. Some of the people whose stories are here came to talk to him about their problem with a son. In most cases, I knew them as well. I have changed their names and jumbled occasional facts about them in order to disguise their identities, because I didn't feel really right about exposing their problem in my book. But I am confident that they would all have wanted their stories told if they believed it would help someone else who is dealing with a similar situation.

I have even changed the names of my own son and his wife and children. Close friends will of course realize who they are, for we have not made a secret of the fact that we have lived with this painful situation for several years. But I wanted to shield them as much as possible, even though I feel that they have wronged us terribly by removing themselves and our grandchildren from the nexus of our relationships.

If you as a reader have suffered from a similar situation, I hope this book will help to console you by showing you how widespread the problem is. You're certainly not in it alone. And I hope too, if you know someone else who is living with a similar impasse in their family relationship, you will pass this book along to them.

I am not sure how your son and daughter-in-law might react if you gave them a copy. I think that if I had had such a book that I hadn't written I might have mailed it to our son and his wife. I would probably have hoped it might shock them into seeing themselves in its pages and cause them to stop treating us the way they have. But I wouldn't have had a lot of confidence in that. Their attitude has seemed unrelievedly cruel, and I doubt if a book like this would have done anything more than infuriate them. You'll have to make your own call about this.

At any rate, this is an honest book about an agonizing problem shared by a lot of people. I haven't cut any corners or fudged any cases. Things are what they are.

My wish for you is simply this, that you will find some relief in knowing that you aren't alone, that there are thousands of us, perhaps hundreds of thousands, who have been tormented by the same behavioral pattern on the part of a beloved son. And as risky as it is, I'm going to give you my e-mail address so you may write to me if you would like to. It's annekillinger@gmail.com. I can't promise to answer every message, but I will try, because I feel deeply about this matter, and can't help thinking how much I wish I'd had somebody to write to when our son and his wife started treating us the way they have—back when Humpty-Dumpty fell off the wall.

                                                              A. K. K.

*This book is dedicated
to all the dear parents
who have lost a son as we have,
not to war or disease or some terrible accident,
but to a woman
who turned out to be the worst enemy
you could have had.*

Humpty-Dumpty sat on a wall,
Humpty-Dumpty had a great fall.
And none of the King's horses,
And none of the King's men,
Could ever put Humpty together again!

— OLD ENGLISH NURSERY RHYME

"You can't fix it."

— DR. ROY WOODRUFF

THAT AWFUL FINAL MEETING

What one hopes, of course, is to keep a
loving relationship with one's own children, with the men and women they
marry and with the grandchildren whom
they produce. All too often this is easier
said than done.

— Mary Stott, *Aging for Beginners*

Oh, this whole day was so sad, the kind
of day when you realize that everyone
eventually got lost from everyone else.

— Anne Tyler, *Breathing Lessons*

It was the worst of times.

— Charles Dickens, *A Tale of Two
Cities*

"I HATE YOU," SAID OUR SON. "I NEVER want to see your faces
again."

Our son was forty-two years old. We thought we had always
had a wonderful relationship. I was a stay-at-home mom, and
did everything I could to give our two boys an ideal childhood.
Their dad, who was a professor during their youth—he would
later become a pastor—spent great chunks of time with them,
taking them swimming, playing tennis and football and basketball, and helping with every imaginable kind of project. We were
a close-knit family.

But there he was, in a restaurant where we had met to talk about what was going on between him and his wife and us, bolting up from the dinner table to make an angry exit. The diners around us gawked at us sympathetically. Maybe they had experienced similar treatment from their own children.

Richard's wife Monica was supposed to have come with him, but she didn't. We weren't surprised. She had begun exhibiting this kind of avoidance several months before they married—showing up late for appointments, sending Richard to make excuses when she was supposed to come to our home for a meal, sometimes ignoring us when she did come. She wanted us to know we were zeroes in her book—or worse, something on the bottom of her shoe—and we usually got the message.

She was Richard's second wife. The first one, Betty Sue, had been the love of his life. She was a cute little blond-headed girl he met in college, and we liked her immensely. But she had changed a lot during their ten years together. She worked for the government and spent a lot of time away from home. The work and her associations at the office made her callous. She was also ambitious, and didn't like it that Richard, who was an artist, made so little money. They didn't have children. She said it would ruin her figure. We weren't surprised when we learned she was leaving Richard.

But it devastated him. He would have done anything to keep her. In fact, he did everything for her even after they separated—helped her find and decorate an apartment, furnished it with some of his own belongings, took her food when she was ill.

We lived three hours away from them at the time. But my husband had semi-retired, and Richard begged us to move nearer, saying he really needed his parents.

So we found another home only thirty minutes from his

and moved. He had dinner with us two or three times a week, and I always sent him home with enough food to last until we saw him again. He was often pensive, but at least we could keep an eye on him and offer moral support.

Then, a couple of years later, he met Monica.

He was eating at a popular young people's pub with a friend. Or his friend was eating. Richard was sitting by him at the bar, cadging an occasional French fry off his plate.

"You'd better not take anything off my plate," said a female voice on his other side, teasing as she crooked her arm around her food.

She was a beautiful girl. Tall, slender, long blond hair, big hazel eyes. I'm sure he felt complimented that she was flirting with him, even though he himself was very attractive and often received attention from women.

When his friend left, he and Monica moved to a table, where they sat eating, drinking, and schmoozing until the wee hours of the morning. During their conversation, he learned that she was ten years younger than he, that she had recently dumped a live-in boyfriend who didn't want to be rehabilitated from a drug habit, and that she was extremely wealthy. Repeat: extremely wealthy. Her grandfather was an incredibly successful businessman who had earned untold millions of dollars. A few years hence, when she would be 36, she was slated to inherit an enormous fortune of her own.

Richard was ecstatic when he called to report that he had met Monica, and he lost no time in bringing her to dinner at our house.

She entranced us that evening with reports of her work as a teacher of autistic children. She was very smart and articulate. She also seemed to care about the children. We were so pleased for Richard that we couldn't hide our happiness over his discovering such a remarkable young woman.

The next day she went away on a trip, and Richard couldn't stop talking about her. When he went to the airport to pick her up on her return, my husband sent a big bouquet of flowers with him that included a "Welcome Home" card with a handwritten message: "Please marry our son!"

It wasn't long before they started living together. Richard had a house, and Monica at first promised to move in with him. But then she talked him into moving into her swanky townhouse and letting a friend stay in his place until he sold it.

A TELLING EVENT

We were invited to the townhouse. Monica was working late and Richard was preparing dinner. He was eager to show us the place, which was on three floors. The lower floor, next to the garage, was the one where Monica's handsome black dog King lived, although he had the run of the entire house.

We sat on a sofa across from the kitchen where Richard was cooking, but King was extremely friendly and wanted our attention. Finally Richard removed him and shut him in his own part of the house.

When Monica came in, she was steamed.

"Why was King shut up down there?" she demanded.

The dog was now with her and prancing about in what I took for canine embarrassment.

"He was interfering with our visiting," Richard explained, "so I closed him up for a while."

"He has the run of the whole house! Don't ever do that again!" Monica announced in a semi-shrill, no-nonsense tone.

Richard didn't say anything. Neither did we.

It was our first glimpse of her imperiousness, and of an unmistakable sense of authority conjoined with what I thought was a very spoiled personality.

After dinner, when the strain had worn off, she showed us scrapbooks of photos of her family, displaying an inordinate pride in her grandfather, the strong, take-charge figure who had built a small business into a vast conglomerate. She obviously had a vivid sense of family, which we thought was right and proper. We didn't realize at the time that we were being measured and found wanting because we didn't have the kind of resources her family did, and, perhaps more importantly, weren't overly impressed by those of her family.

Bit by bit, we learned about the rest of her family. Her mother and father were divorced. Her brother and only sibling worked for the grandfather's company, as had her father. When her father and mother divorced, her father had worked for the company a number of years, so was given a handsome settlement, plus an annual "salary" that was quite spectacular in itself. Now in his early fifties, he had a big house on Florida's Gulf Coast and lived there most of the year. Her mother also owned a house in Florida, and spent winters in it.

We went home that night feeling very ordinary. Monica certainly had an interesting family. We also talked about the display of temper we had seen over the incident with the dog. But we weren't in any way dissuaded from supporting her and Richard's relationship, and were as excited as any parents could be when we learned a couple of months later that he had given her a ring.

My husband was pastoring a resort church on Mackinac Island, Michigan, during the summer months, and that summer we invited Richard to bring Monica for a visit. It was a very happy visit and she seemed to love the quirky, beautiful little island. Especially the clothing shops, which she frequented almost every day, coming in with shopping bags filled with expensive items.

They told us during their visit that they had set their wedding date for a year later, because it was to be a very big affair and would require a lot of preparation.

Our excitement about the wedding, unfortunately, was quickly deflated after we returned home and began seeing Richard and Monica more regularly. Invariably, when we had a date for lunch or dinner, she would either come in her own car and be late or, if she came with Richard, would make him late as well. She didn't seem to have a punctuality problem about most things, but somehow she always did with us, as if she were reminding us that she was important enough to be waited on.

At Christmas, we made a point of finding nice gifts for both of them. Our gift from Monica, however, was a box of the Christmas dishes her mother had bought for all the employees in her business. We had seen them when Monica discovered them one night in a drug store on sale for ten dollars a set and had immediately cell-phoned her mother to tell her about them.

THE FITTING

A couple of months later, though, I was thrilled when Monica asked if I would go with her for the fitting of her wedding dress. Her mother was in Florida for the winter, and I was to be her other mother for this special occasion. When I met her at the bridal boutique, however, her mother had flown back from Florida to be there, and I realized in the course of the fitting that the only reason they wanted me along was to guide me in the choice of my own dress for the wedding.

I looked at the dresses on the mother-in-law's rack, most of which were extraordinarily expensive. I had never paid $500 for a garment, even if it was a very fancy suit, and most of the dresses in this collection were at least twice that. So I tactfully suggested that I would wait until the spring and summer dresses had all come in and there would be a better selection.

"All right," said Monica's mother. "But don't buy anything until we've had a chance to see it."

It wasn't a suggestion. It was a command.

Two weeks later, my husband and other son and I saw another bridal store in a shopping mall and found a beautiful aubergine dress with a pattern of aubergine beads on the skirt, and it was only $300. I tried it on and my husband and son both loved it, so I bought it. I also went to a fabric store and found some matching beads so I could carry the pattern onto the back of the dress, and I applied the same beads to an aubergine purse, so they would look as if they were created for one another. I hung the dress on the rack on the door of our laundry room, and the next time Richard and Monica came to our home I could barely wait to show it to them.

Monica took one look at it and said, "Oh."

Richard discreetly said nothing.

We felt an increasing chilliness in the atmosphere whenever they were around, but plowed on, thinking it would all warm up after they married. Easter was coming, and we were pleased that Richard asked if they could have Easter dinner with us, inasmuch as Monica's mother would still be in Florida.

"Of course," we said, "what times suits you?"

Richard, knowing we usually had the midday meal between twelve and twelve-thirty, suggested one o'clock.

We said fine. We looked forward to it. Easter was always a special day in our family life.

A PLACE FOR THE REHEARSAL DINNER

One of the places where we had been feeling tension with Richard and Monica—especially Monica—was over the rehearsal dinner for their wedding. My husband thought, inasmuch as the wedding was to be at a location in downtown Washington, DC, that a dinner a few blocks away at Old Ebbitt Grill, a fine historic dining place that had often catered to presidents, was a natural, because everybody could simply walk there. But for some reason she refused to explain, Monica wanted it to be near her home in the suburbs, which would entail everybody's driving through heavy traffic for an hour or two to get there.

We took the two of them to Ebbitt for lunch one Sunday so they could see how fine a place it was and what good food they served. But after we ate and one of the managers came to show us the spaces available for a big dinner, Monica excused herself to go to the bathroom and didn't return for more than half an hour, as we were finishing the tour. We tried to share our enthusiasm with her, but she was very dismissive. It was clear that she wasn't interested in having the dinner there.

The next week they took us to a resort hotel near Monica's home and indicated that they favored it, as we could easily seat 250 or 300 guests there. Whoa, we thought! Rehearsal dinners are for wedding participants, immediate family, and close friends, not for all the wedding guests. We knew about weddings and rehearsal dinners, because we had been to hundreds of each, most of them conducted by my husband. But Monica wanted a huge crowd, and the prices at the resort were astronomical.

We finally settled on another restaurant near her home, where the space was quite attractive and the prices less exorbitant. Our son also agreed that we could hold the number of guests down to "about a hundred," although Monica wasn't saying anything. We paid a deposit and calculated that the whole business was going to cost about $25,000, which still seemed excessive to us, especially in view of the fact that there would be a gala wedding dinner the following day.

At some point in all of this, Richard and Monica informed us that her brother was preparing the program for the rehearsal dinner, and its centerpiece would be a slide show of her old family pictures. John and I were stunned. Everything was centered on her, and not on her new life with Richard. Richard was going along as if it didn't matter to him. We had the feeling that we were being mugged by experts. I don't know how we managed to suppress our growing uneasiness about everything, but somehow we did.

THE BIG BLOW-UP

Then, a few days before Easter, Richard e-mailed me to say that Monica wanted to have Easter brunch with her brother and his partner and therefore they'd like to come to our place for dinner about four.

I e-mailed back, trying to stifle my resentment, and suggested that we have dinner another time, as they appeared to be quite busy on Easter. I think I reminded him that his father had never eaten Easter dinner at four in the afternoon and wouldn't be too pleased at the idea.

Richard responded with a heated message in which he said I had never loved him or considered his happiness.

My husband, upset with his response, e-mailed him to remind him that before he was born I had refused to have my pregnancy terminated when he attempted to abort, and had gone to bed for weeks in order to keep him. How could he say I had never loved him? John also let loose some of his pent-up feelings about the way Monica was leading him around by the nose and producing almost constant tension in our family relationship.

"You are marrying into a wealthy and powerful family," he wrote, "and if you don't start standing up to Monica now in behalf of yourself and your family, you may one day find yourself in a very deferential position, walking, like Prince Philip, a few paces behind the rest of the family."

We did not realize at the time, but learned later, that Monica was reading all Richard's e-mails and helping him compose the replies she thought he ought to make. We could only imagine, when we did discover this, how this particular e-mail got up her nose, as the British say. In fact, she would later openly and bitterly refer to the way my husband had insulted her family in that particular e-mail.

In the early days of their engagement, Richard and Monica had asked my husband to perform their wedding. He was very experienced with weddings, as he performed about fifty each summer at the Little Stone Church on Mackinac Island and had even published a book of Contemporary Wedding Services a few years earlier. Soon after they asked him to do their wedding,

he set about writing a special service for it, alluding not only to
their individual qualities but to the setting in the museum, and
presented it to them at Christmas for their approval.

We noticed at the time that they said nothing, but supposed
they simply had their minds on something else. When he asked
Richard a few weeks later how they had liked the wedding service he had written, Richard said that Monica didn't think it was
personal enough. My husband was amazed, because he had
never made a service quite so thoroughly personal.

A couple of weeks after the brouhaha over Easter, he received a letter from Richard—a very formal act for someone
who almost never wrote a letter—saying that he and Monica
had decided to ask someone else who would be "less biased" to
perform their wedding, and that he knew his father would be
relieved because he could sit with his wife at a wedding for a
change.

My husband was hurt and I was very angry.

We e-mailed Richard and said we needed to meet and talk.
He replied that he wouldn't have time until after the wedding—
which was still nearly three months away. We tried to phone but
both he and Monica, who had caller ID and could see in ad-
vance who was calling, avoided our attempts to reach them.

Finally, in exasperation, I wrote Richard and said that in
view of their feelings about his father's "bias," maybe it would
be better if we didn't come to their wedding at all. We would
be on Mackinac Island for the summer, anyway, and would have
to come back. And I admit I was still smarting a bit that they
had decided not to attend a big fiftieth anniversary party my
husband I were planning at the Grand Hotel on the island because they would be "too busy." We would pay for the rehearsal
dinner as planned, I said. In fact, we had already made a sizable
deposit on it. But we would merely send our best wishes for the

day of the nuptials.

Richard's reply—or Monica's, by dictation—was formal and bloodless. We should do as we felt best, but, he added at the end, "You will always be welcome at our wedding."

We couldn't believe we had painted ourselves into a corner and they wouldn't rescue us. Surely, I thought, they would be horrified at the suggestion that we might not attend, and would insist that we come. And we still thought, when we packed up and moved to Mackinac for the summer, that they'd relent and ask us to be there. Or, if they didn't, her mother would surely write and say they wanted us there.

But no letter or phone call ever came.

A well-meaning friend insisted that we ought to return home and show up at the wedding anyway. She said we'd always regret it if we didn't. But we honestly didn't feel welcome. I'd have walked on broken glass to get there if they had even written to suggest that we attend and they would miss us if we didn't. As it was—well, we felt written out, excluded.

On the day of their wedding, which was a Saturday and meant that my husband had a couple of weddings to perform at the Little Stone Church, we rose early, walked up into the woods at the center of the island, dug a little hole in the ground, and buried their photograph as a ritual of exorcism to put the whole business behind us. Maybe it was a juvenile thing to do, but we thought it might make us feel better. That evening, after John's weddings, we had dinner at the Grand Hotel with our other son, Eric, and toasted the future happiness of the newly married couple. I had tears in my eyes, and I think I saw one or two at the corners of John's eyes as well.

The rest of the summer and the fall passed. I kept hoping at Christmas that Richard would relent and get in touch with us. I always called him "my Christmas child" because he loved the holidays so much. When he was young, he started singing carols before the end of summer, and we often made new Christmas gifts and decorations long before the season arrived. I didn't see how he could stay away from home at Christmas.

But he did.

It was all I could do to keep from calling him or driving to their house and ringing the doorbell. But at the same time I felt so unwanted that I was miserable, and knew it wouldn't do any good to try to contact them. If they wanted to see us, they would make the move.

John wrote them a sweet, tender letter at Christmas, saying we missed them and would love to be with them when we could.

They didn't answer.

The winter months passed. Still nothing. Then the spring, and it was time for us to pack and return to Mackinac.

RAPPROCHEMENT?

That summer, a routine X-ray revealed a small spot on one of John's lungs, and a doctor friend advised that he have it removed surgically, as he had had a melanoma several years before and we couldn't be too careful now. We scheduled the operation in Detroit in mid-September.

It was supposed to be a routine procedure. The surgeon would make a three-inch incision below John's shoulder blade on the right side, go in, snip out the tissue where the spot was, and test it. If it was all right, he would sew up the incision and that would be that.

But for some reason, the doctor cut a ten-inch opening and removed an entire lobe of the lung, plus another bit at the bottom. Later, when we asked for the X-rays and surgical notes to take to our doctor back home, we were told they had been misplaced. "It happens all the time in the OR," an office worker told us. It doesn't, of course. We have since learned that it is illegal to lose such records, and have concluded that the surgeon got John's X-rays mixed up with someone else's and cut far more than was necessary. The pathologist's report, which we fought for weeks to acquire, was negative. The spot was probably a calcium deposit or some kind of scar.

John took the operation in stride, and was soon walking around the hospital corridors, pulling his tube trolley with him.

But four days after surgery he bent to retrieve a pillow that had fallen from his bed to the floor, and when he did he couldn't get his breath. It was Sunday, and things at the hospital were slow. But it was soon determined that he had had a large shower of emboli in his lungs. A sonogram found massive clots behind his knees. That evening, when one of the hospital surgeons had returned from his weekend away, he installed a Greenfield filter in John's vena cava, a sort of clothless umbrella whose antennae would catch large clots trying to travel up the main artery to the heart and lungs. Eric, his wife Pia, and I were told to go back to our motel and get some rest, as he would be in ICU all night and we couldn't stay. They gave John a 40 percent chance of recovery.

John and I kissed as I prepared to leave, and both of us fought back tears. "Call Richard," his last words to me were, "and tell him I love him."

I didn't want to call, but I steeled myself to do it. Amazingly, Richard answered, probably because I was calling from an out-of-state number he didn't recognize. I tried to tell him what was happening, but he said he couldn't understand me because my speech was garbled. I was crying and trying to talk at the same time, and apparently my words were incomprehensible.

Finally, I got enough control of myself to tell him his father might not make it through the night and wanted him to know he loved him.

Two days later, on Tuesday, Richard and Monica showed up at the hospital. I stood back as they went to John's side to say hello. Monica was all smiles. I guessed why. She was clearly and triumphantly pregnant.

John cried when she told him. It would be our first grandchild.

They stayed two or three hours, then said they had to catch their plane home. Richard was a schoolteacher and had to be back in the classroom the next day.

"It has been worth my surgery and the problem with the clots," John said, "if this has brought us all back together again."

It did and it didn't.

OUR NEW "TOGETHERNESS"

When we got home from Detroit, we started seeing them every week or two for a meal or a drop-by visit. They had built an enormous new home, and were eager to show it to us because they were very proud of it. Richard, who was an artist, had painted the new baby's room to be a little girl's paradise, because they had learned that the little newcomer would be a female. And Richard had an art studio added to the original plans for the house.

It was his studio, but Monica had had a bank of bookshelves, cabinets, and a computer desk built at one end of it for herself. Richard wasn't going to have it all to himself, even though the house was immense and Monica could have chosen any of a dozen other places for her own study.

When Abigail was born, a few days after Christmas, we were invited to the hospital. Her family had already been there, and her brother had filmed the birth. In fact, he was so emotionally involved that in some ways it seemed like it was his child who had arrived, not Richard and Monica's.

For the first year of Abigail's life, we were often included in parties, family get-togethers, and other events. Monica even invited us to attend Abigail's Gymboree class when she was nine months old, and see her moving to music with the other children, all of whom were considerably older than she. It was clear that Monica was already programming her daughter's life in a big way. She had also enrolled her in a swimming class.

I got to participate in my son's family's life more than I expected that year because Abigail was allergic to her mother's milk when Monica ate certain foods. So I volunteered to fix whatever she needed and wanted to eat, and frequently took in whole dinners that could be reheated for two or three meals. I had never been happier than I was while doing something for my family again.

We loved little Abby. She had red hair and looked exactly like my husband when he was her age. The two of them seemed to have a very simpatico relationship, too, as if she recognized some deep kinship between them even at her tender age.

I'll never forget the evening we were babysitting so her parents could go out for an anniversary dinner. There was a great thunderstorm, and the lightning flashed brilliantly from one part of the sky to another, always followed by huge thunderclaps. Abby seemed to be afraid, just as her mother was whenever there was a storm.

John took her out into a sunroom where they were surrounded by glass, and they sat very near to one another on the sofa. John spoke excitedly to her about how the noise always followed the flashes, and would say, "Ah, there's a big flash over there! Listen, now, Abby. Let's hear the thunder!" And when the thunder came, he would laugh uproariously. Soon she was mimicking him, and the two of them were watching keenly for the next bolt of lightning so they could crack up when the thunder rolled. I knew she would never again be afraid of thunderstorms, no matter how long she lived.

Abigail was followed 19 months later by little Rachel. Monica had Rachel by induced labor, and she and Richard asked us to come to their house the morning they were to go to the hospital so we could stay with Abigail. John suggested that we come the night before so we would be on hand whenever they wanted to leave.

"No," said Monica, "my father and his girl friend are here. You and Anne come about ten. Then I want you to bring Abby to the hospital after I've had Rachel."

The traffic was heavy between our house and theirs, and we were 15 minutes late. Her father and his friend barely spoke to us when we arrived. They were obviously miffed about our being late, as they said they had scheduled some massages, to which they rushed off almost immediately.

We played with Abby and gave her her lunch. We waited and waited for word from the hospital, but it didn't come.

Finally, about three that afternoon, Monica's father and his friend came in. They had talked with Monica on their cell phones and said the baby had arrived. John said great, we would take Abby down to meet her baby sister.

"That won't be necessary," said Monica's dad. "They wanted us to bring Abby with us. Monica said you could go on home."

Hurt, but unwilling to show it, we appeared at the hospital the following day with gifts for the new mother and her two daughters. Richard was holding the baby and Monica was in the bathroom putting on makeup. I wanted to hold the baby, but Richard obviously had orders that I shouldn't. He kept her across the room from us and made nervous talk until Monica finally emerged from the bathroom 20 or 30 minutes later.

We tried to be cheerful and pointed out the gaily wrapped presents we had brought. She reacted sullenly and unemotionally, and didn't move to open them. She picked up one, looked at it, then threw it onto the bed and left it unopened. A few minutes later, we beat our retreat, feeling once more hurt and humiliated.

Again we didn't know what we had done or said, but we were clearly in the doghouse for something.

Nor did we ever get out.

They managed to keep us at arm's length from then on. I think I got to see and hold my second granddaughter a total of five times in the next six or seven months, and never for more than five minutes at a time. It was as if I weren't trusted to cradle her, lest I would drop her or try to rush out the door with her.

We puzzled and puzzled over what had happened this time, but could never figure it out.

THE SHOWDOWN, IF IT COULD BE CALLED THAT

Finally, after frequent turndowns, they agreed to come to our home for a birthday dinner for Richard two days before his actual forty-second birthday. We didn't think much about the fact that we never got to celebrate their birthdays with any of them on the actual dates; those were always reserved for her family. But this one was to be a fateful day. John had resolved to confront Richard and Monica about why they were so cool toward us and wouldn't let us have more time with our grand-children. Our other son Eric and his wife Pia were also present.

We had barely finished the big meal I prepared and Richard had blown out the candles on his cake and opened the presents we gave him before Monica announced that they needed to leave because she had something else to do that afternoon.

I said, "Before you go, your dad wants to talk with you about something."

Puzzled, they followed us into the den. I was playing with Abby and Monica was carrying Rachel, who had popped off to sleep after eating.

John began by saying he wanted to talk about the elephant in the room, the one that had been there a long time. We were growing older, he said, and felt terrible that we didn't have a closer relationship to our children, even though we all lived so near to one another. He said we especially grieved about not seeing our grandchildren more often and for more quality ex-periences.

At this point, Abby was becoming distracting, so I took her upstairs to allow the others to talk. John said Monica pretty much took the floor at this point and began spouting off about all the things she didn't like about us. Among the things she re-sented about me, she said, was that when I was preparing meals for them I had once got Richard on the phone and asked him what she would like to eat.

"She should have asked me," she insisted shrilly. "It was none of Richard's business what I wanted!"

John thought Richard was actually relieved that he was giv-ing Monica a chance to spout off, possibly because he thought it would relieve the tension between us and things would be better.

The conversation went on for more than an hour. I tried to

keep Abby entertained, and was worn out by the time the exchange in the den ended and John called to say Richard and Monica and the children were leaving.

I don't know why, but as they were gathering up their things to leave, I held out my arms to little Abby and said, "Abby, come give Grammy a big hug to last her the rest of her life!"

She did, squeezing me around the neck until her little eyes bulged. I don't know if I was being prescient or what, but I had the feeling that I would never see her again.

I didn't, and it has been more than four years since that day.

As they left, John thanked them for coming and said he hoped we could get together within a few days to continue the talking that had begun in our den. But for the next two or three months they ignored our calls and didn't answer a single one of our many e-mails.

Finally Richard picked up on one of John's calls. John was totally shocked at the hostility in his voice and attitude. He said he was really abusive, and that it wasn't the same man who had been at our house before his birthday. But Richard agreed that he and Monica would meet us for lunch at a restaurant not far from where they lived.

We didn't know what to expect as we settled into a booth at the restaurant to wait for them. Then we saw Richard drive up outside. Monica was not with him. He strode into the restaurant and took a seat opposite us.

"Dad," he blurted out, "I don't know why you wanted to have this meeting. There isn't going to be a reconciliation. I don't know why I came. This really upsets me!"

We couldn't understand this strange hostility. What had happened since that day at our house a few months earlier? Were these Richard's own feelings or was his behavior being dictated by Monica?

We asked repeatedly what we had done that had created such animosity in him.

"You know what you've done!" he said.

But we honestly didn't. If we had known, we might have been able to offer an explanation or deal with his blatant anger.

"Who is this man?" I kept asking myself. This couldn't possibly be our fun-loving, adorable son who used to announce every morning at the breakfast table that this was going to be the happiest day of his life.

My husband kept looking him in the eye and asking him to be specific about what we'd done to offend him and Monica so grievously.

"You just don't get it, do you, Dad?" he said. "You never get it. I tried to tell you in my e-mails how I felt, and that's all I'm going to say."

"What doesn't your dad get?" I asked.

"There you go, Mom," he said, "—making faces!"

Maybe I looked bewildered, but I didn't realize I was making faces. I simply couldn't understand what was transpiring.

"Son," I pled, "I'm not making faces. Maybe I look stunned. That's possible. I just can't grasp what's happening, and what's making you behave this way."

"You're doing it again," he said. "You're treating me like a small boy and you are not going to manipulate me! That's why I never like to talk to you. You always try to manipulate me, and I hate it!"

I looked at his father in astonishment.

"There you go again, Mom," he said bitterly. "You're making faces and looking at Dad."

We could only shake our heads and feel helpless.

"You never just drop by to see us," he said.

That was a corker. "We never feel welcome to do that," I

said. "You're always in such a hurry to get rid of us that we try not to bother you unless it's a scheduled event."

His anger continued to mount. "You wanted Rachel to be a boy!" he shouted.

"What do you mean?" I gasped.

"You know," he said. "We have the e-mail to prove it."

I shook my head. I knew I had never said or written anything like that. In the beginning, we were told that the child Monica was carrying was a boy and that they were going to name him Riley. Then a subsequent ultrasound revealed that Riley was in fact a girl, not a boy. But I knew I hadn't ever disparaged the child because she wasn't a boy.

Later, when we got home from the restaurant, I called up the old e-mail he had referred to, and saw what I'd actually written. I had said I'd hesitated writing about their discovery that they were having a girl because I was trying to get used to the change.

"I hope you and Richard aren't too disappointed," I said to Monica. "I know you didn't mind which sex your baby would be, but it must be hard to have to switch gears. I know Richard had the plans all drawn up for a boy's room. But now he can enjoy changing things for Rachel. There is a purpose for everything, and it is meant for you to have not one, but two wonderful daughters. We are grateful."

And I signed the e-mail "Love, Anne."

We couldn't believe our meeting at the restaurant could have gone so badly. Richard was clearly in an emotional crisis of some kind, and wasn't about to grant us an inch of leeway.

Finally he leapt up, his food unfinished, and threw down some bills by his plate to pay for it.

His dad told him he would take care of it.

"Not for me," he said. "I pay my own way."

This was when he told us he hated us and never wanted to see us again. then he turned and strode toward the door, leaving us in a state of total shock.

Just as he reached the door, he swung around and returned.

"Oh, thank God," I thought, "he's coming back. He's going to apologize."

That wasn't his intention.

"I'll give you one thing," he spat at us. "I had a wonderful childhood. Look how well I turned out!"

And he spun on his heels and headed out again.

They say one's sense of humor lies very close to a sense of total despair. As blitzed as we were, I couldn't help turning to John and saying, "Look how well your son turned out."

How Could It Happen?

> We alone of all the creatures look around at our children, glance at the shadows, listen to the sounds of the neighborhood, and laugh, or sing, or weep.
>
> — Christopher de Vinck, *Only the Heart Knows How to Find Them*

> What had gone wrong? What had become of the babies she had borne and loved and brought up and educated and generally cared for?
>
> — Rosamunde Pilcher, *The Shell Seekers*

> How sharper than a serpent's tooth it is To have a thankless child.
>
> — William Shakespeare, *King Lear*

I'VE PLAYED IT OVER AND OVER again, trying to figure out where everything went wrong. Every parent does at a time like this. You revisit your children's lives and remember things you thought you had long ago forgotten. You turn over the ashes of the past, sifting for clues, looking for some kind of reasonable explanation for what has happened. What did you miss in your child's life that might explain this unexpected behavior today?

I remembered a hot, sultry day in August 1963. John and I were living in Princeton, New Jersey. We had taken our two-year-old son Eric and gone to Kroger's. He let me out at the door and went to find a parking place. Before he had even driven out of sight, something went through my body. It wasn't exactly a shock wave, and it wasn't terribly painful. But it happened, and I felt it. Then there was blood trickling down my inner thighs.

I was panicked! I walked round in circles, not knowing if I could hold on till John came back. I felt so helpless. A man standing nearby saw my distress. As my eyes met his, I called out to him.

"Help me, please!" I begged. "I'm losing my baby!"

The man picked me up and carried me into the store, where a manager instantly recognized what was happening and directed us to the employee's lounge, where there was a sofa. He laid me down gently. There were several women in the lounge when we went in. I'm still amazed at their presence of mind. One got some paper towels to help catch the blood. Another elevated my feet. A third got on the public-address system and called for my husband to come to the lounge.

Soon John was bending over me, speaking in soothing tones, and providing the strength and comfort I needed.

I had never been so scared in my life. I wanted that baby. I had to have that baby. I would not abort it. My mind was already made up. We had to save our child!

John brought the car around and sped me to the local hospital. We went to the emergency entrance. The doors were thrown open and I was rushed to the operating room.

Someone at the grocery store had called my doctor, and he was there within a few minutes of our own arrival. When he had examined me, he shook his head.

"We'll have to abort the fetus," he said. "It's too dangerous to let it go to term."

I disagreed. I wanted to carry my baby. I loved my baby!

My doctor argued with me. "You can hemorrhage and bleed to death," he explained.

In the end, my weeping and stubbornness convinced him to let me try to keep the fetus. I was assigned a room at the hospital. He said he would return in the morning to check on me.

It was a long, difficult night. John had gotten a sitter to stay with Eric so he could visit me until it was time for the sitter to leave. I was afraid to move even slightly. I lay in the same position until I thought I would turn to stone, but I didn't want to give that little embryo another thought about coming out. I was afraid to even sneeze or cough, lest it be the end of my struggle, and I prayed without ceasing. John had a little spoken prayer and kissed me before he left.

The doctor returned very early the next morning. I imagined he expected he would have to put me in the OR and take the fetus, and he would do it in plenty of time to get to his office for the other patients.

We exchanged the usual pleasantries. He wanted to know if I had been able to sleep and how I was feeling. He asked if I had been up at all during the night. Then he examined me.

There was a look of amazement on his face. The bleeding had stopped, he said, and all my vital signs looked good. He seemed to be carrying on an argument with himself about whether he should go ahead and perform an abortion.

But apparently he remembered how insistent I had been.

"I guess you can go home," he said, "and we'll see how it goes. But you're going to have to stay in bed a lot and get plenty of rest. Don't lift anything heavy. Stay in touch with my office. If you need anything, call."

I was delighted to follow his orders. Anything to keep my baby!

We were moving to Louisville shortly after this episode, where my husband would become academic dean of a college. It was the only time in a lifetime of moving that I didn't have to turn a hand. My husband and a lady from our church packed everything and cleaned the house as we prepared to leave for our new home.

A few months later, Richard was born. He was a jaundiced baby and had to stay in the hospital a couple of extra days because of that, but otherwise he was fine. The jaundice made him extremely fussy, but we understood that and tried to be patient.

A HAPPY BACKGROUND

There was never a more independent child. When Richard was two and it was time to teach him to tie his shoes, he pulled away from us, saying, "I do myself!" And he did.

When he was three, we took him to Paris, France, where my husband was visiting theologian-in-residence at the American Church and was writing a book on the theater of the absurd. He attended a bilingual nursery school attended primarily by French students. His teacher said he picked up French quickly, yet refused to converse in it. When we asked him about this, he replied, "I not Flinch and I not speak Flinch!"

His hair was blond in those early years, and grew in ringlets that bobbed up and down when he walked or ran. He always seemed to be in motion, and was a daredevil about everything. He took so many chances on his bicycle and the little cars and scooters he had, plunging them over hills and drop-offs at reckless speeds, that we sometimes wondered if he would survive into his teenage years.

He was only three or four when he began to exhibit remarkable drawing talent, and it was soon obvious that he would grow up to be a cartoonist or a painter. Once, when he was about six, we took him and his brother to the Prado, the great Spanish museum filled with paintings of a religious nature, especially the crucifixion of Jesus. Afterward, as we drove along in our car, he showed me a drawing he had just made. It was of Jesus on the cross, and there was a figure kneeling nearby with great teardrops falling from her face.

"Who is that?" I asked, pointing to the figure.

"That's his mother," said Richard. "Don't you know it hurted her?"

Now I wonder if he even understands what really hurts mothers.

He was sometimes a challenge as a youngster, to his teachers and to us as well, but both his teachers and we knew he was worth it.

Fiercely competitive, he was a terror on the playing field and didn't like to be beaten at anything. Whenever we engaged in a family game of Monopoly, he invariably ended up overheating, so that his face turned red, and he would eventually get so mad at gambling some big property and losing it that he cried and went away angry.

He broke more than one tennis racket when he played with his dad, who wasn't nearly as athletic a player but usually managed to eke out a victory by being calm and resourceful. Richard often complained afterward about his dad's "dinky little drop shots."

His classmates adored him, and he was a born leader. He won so many prizes at his eight-grade graduation—"Most Popular," "Best GPA," "Best Athlete," "Best Actor," etc.—that we actually became embarrassed when his name was called again.

By this time, he had become highly socialized, for he man-

aged to get along well with all sorts of people and was invariably
the anointed spokesman for whatever group he was in, either at
school or at church.

His one disappointment seemed to be that he hadn't developed a fabulous torso to go with his limitless energy and upbeat
personality. Occasionally we would catch glimpses of him going
shirtless around our contemporary house in the summer time
and stopping to flex his muscles in front of the big windows
where he could see his reflection. But by the time he got to college, he had begun to build those muscles, and, with a 46-inch
chest and 30-inch waist, standing six-feet-one, and boasting a
face like a movie star, he was a veritable Adonis of a man.

He seemed to enjoy college and came out with a *cum laude*
degree in spite of the fact that he spent most of his time on his
art, his friends, and courting Betty Sue, the girl he would marry,
not on his studies. We liked Betty Sue, who was a year behind
him, and were glad they had found one another. She came from
a good family and we thought she was a good influence on him.

When he graduated, he moved near her parents and took a
job with an art firm in Washington, DC, to wait for her to graduate.

Despite a hiccup during that year because she liked dating
other boys on campus, they eventually married, and my husband
performed the wedding service. Betty Sue got a job with the
government, we helped them with the down payment on a new
house in the suburbs, and they seemed to be extremely happy.

It wasn't long, though, before a streak of venality began to
show itself in Betty Sue. She was earning a good salary but
wasn't happy with Richard's income as an artist. She thought he
should be selling fine paintings, and proposed that we supple-
ment his income for a period in which he would devote himself
to producing the kind of works that would establish him in the

art world. My husband, always eager to help his children, acquiesced, and drew up a contract with Richard that called for us to pay him $3,000 a month for 36 months. The original paintings would belong to us, but we would also pay for making prints, and, when our cost on each had been satisfied, all profits would belong to him.

I think Richard was very happy during this period. He created some outstanding paintings, and he and Betty Sue appeared to get along beautifully. But when the prints did not sell as readily as expected, her disappointment was obvious, and we could tell their relationship was deteriorating. So we weren't totally shocked when they began talking divorce. Nor were we surprised when she appeared to be vindictive and wanted to take him for everything they had, including their house.

Richard's situation was precarious. Betty Sue plowed much of her salary into her own retirement account, while they had lived on the money he managed to earn. So when she sued for divorce he was virtually penniless. We stepped in at that point and hired the person recommended to us as the best divorce lawyer in the area. As expensive as she was, she was worth it, because she saved his house, his furnishings, and his car.

But Richard was deeply hurt. He had really loved Betty Sue, and he felt betrayed. He admitted to us that she was probably having an affair with someone in her department at work. We did our best to support and encourage him, and assured him of our loyalty during what would be a trying time as he attempted to reestablish his life without her.

It was at this point that he asked us to move nearer to him and we did. He worked as a teacher in his local high school, and was promoted to chairman of a seven-person art department. And a year or two later, he met Monica on that fateful evening at the pub.

A PROMISING BEGINNING AND A TRAGIC ENDING

As I said, we were delighted when they hooked up. She was a lovely girl, she seemed to be devoted to her work with autistic children, and she had so much money that Richard would be able to pursue his art work without any financial worries.

We had no idea, when their romance began, what it would do to tear up our family relationship. We knew that such things happen. They always have. Even the Bible, as old as it is, says, "Those who do violence to their father and chase away their mother are children who cause shame and bring reproach" (Proverbs 19:26). And there is that finely written passage near the beginning of Jane Austen's *Sense and Sensibility*, first published in 1811, about the way young John Dashwood's greedy and imperious wife, Mrs. Dashwood, immediately installed herself and her son at Norland, the family estate, once John's father had died, and began craftily whittling away at John's noble intention of awarding each of his three half-sisters a thousand pounds for annual living expenses until he ended by giving them nothing more than his good wishes as they and their mother—his step-mother—were packed off to live in a simple cottage offered by a relation in faraway Devonshire.

Austen found this controlling woman so obnoxious that she didn't even deign to bestow a first name on her!

Our son had been so happy with us, and so eager to have us near him, that we could not have believed, when he first met Monica, that she could so distort his opinion of us and destroy his loyalty to us and his brother Eric that he would end by reviling us and saying he never wished to lay eyes on us again. But that is precisely what happened.

Like Mrs. Dashwood, Monica was very crafty. Indeed, she was so ingenious that we were a long time figuring out what had happened to our relationship with Richard. It was only afterward, when we began piecing together the various clues, from her deliberate tardiness at family gatherings to her disdain of my dress for the wedding to our discovery that she had been reading and dictating the answers to our e-mail correspondence with our son, that we began to realize how masterfully she had taken control of our son's life, of his very soul, so that she and not he was directing their every move in our relationship.

For a year or two, we kept theorizing that either Richard was having a nervous breakdown or had a tumor on his brain that was compelling him to behave in complete opposition to his original character. He had been such a wise, good-natured person before he met Monica. He had loved us with all the appropriate fealty of a son who had been well treated and much loved all of his life. I always received Mother's Day cards that proclaimed me the best mother in the world, and his father received comparable accolades on Father's Day. He went out of his way to find little tokens of affection that revealed his genuine care for us. So we could not at first help thinking something drastic had happened to his mind.

One day, when we were attending my high school class reunion in our home town, my husband happened to sit by the son of one of my classmates, a fine young man who had gone through a period of drug addiction, committed himself to a rehabilitation program, and afterwards gone into the field of drug counseling. In the course of their conversation, John briefly described our situation with Richard and asked if it sounded to him as if our son might be having a drug problem. He thought about it for a minute and said no, he didn't think so, unless Richard was exhibiting signs of difficulty in his work or other relationships.

"But," he continued, "have you ever considered mind control?"

"Mind control?" echoed John.

He nodded. He had done a good bit of study in the psychology of mind control, he said, as part of his coming to grips with the matter of why people take drugs for the first time. The radical turnaround in our son's behavior, he suggested, might be from his wife's effect on him. Maybe she was requiring this puzzling behavior of him.

John continued to think about this. When we returned home, he got on the Internet and began looking up material on mind control. What he found astounded him. The same techniques that apply to the manipulation of a person in a group or cult, according to all the authorities on mind control, apply to individuals with "battered person syndrome." And battered person syndrome is a category extending far beyond our usual picture of it, that of a beaten, humiliated spouse or child. It also applies to perfectly normal looking people who are being mercilessly controlled by a parent, a spouse, an employer, or even a close friend.

John compiled a list of common techniques in mind control, which I shall provide in italics. My own comments follow in ordinary print:

> (1) *Take charge of the individual's environment, both physically and emotionally.* I thought of Monica's inducing Richard to leave his house and move into her condo, where she dictated the movements of everything, even her dog King, and of the way she had intruded upon his studio in the new home, installing herself and her computer in one end of it, despite the size of the house and other available places.

(2) Take over the individual's time, totally and exclusively.
In the months before Richard and Monica's marriage,
he told us he didn't have time to see us until after the
wedding. When we did see them, she always said
when it was time to go. He was always as closely gov-
erned as a prisoner in a cell, and his time was never his
to spend as he might have wished.

*(3) Define the individual's former patterns and situations as
irrelevant or evil. Remind him or her constantly of the
inherently bad things about them and rehearse these as
often as possible. Make the person glad to be in a new
situation.* Of course that's what she was doing! It explained the tension we felt when we were around him.
He was being reprogrammed to despise his old life
and conditioned to accept his new one. It is why, on
the day we had his last birthday lunch with us and
began to reminisce about the good times we had when
he was a child, he said he couldn't recall any of them
now. And why else would he have said his father was
"biased" and couldn't perform their marriage ceremony? Monica belonged to a broken family of lapsed
Roman Catholics. Perhaps she taught our son to
think of his father, a highly respected Protestant minister, as representing some kind of sinister faith that
takes advantage of its adherents.

*(4) If the individual asks questions, turn them on the person
in such a way as to make him or her appear wrong, unfaithful, and ungrateful for even asking them.* I bet she
was doing this too. She was training Richard to be
grateful for what she was giving him—life in a big
house, comfort, sex, trips to Florida in the family
plane, acceptance in her family, all the money he

would ever need.

(5) Train the individual to accept your closed system of logic and authoritative structures as right, and to know that you do not tolerate feedback or accept modification of them. Our son had been kidnapped and indoctrinated in a wholly new system, one where she was the good guy and we were the bad guys.

(6) Provide incentives for "good" behavior and punishment for "bad" behavior. I remember how our son Eric reported after a visit in their home before they married that Richard had differed with Monica about something and she had threatened to withhold his "sexual pleasures." She made it sound playful, but Eric could tell there was an edge to her threat. There were of course many other incentives to radical obedience: a new car every few months, the approval of her family, great vacations, her continuing good will, and, after they began having children, the joy of their own little family.

(7) Teach the individual early on that he or she must ask permission for all major decisions as they arise and always follow his or her leader's directives. Here I thought of what I'd observed about Richard's work as chairman of the art department in his high school. Monica had taken over the role of hostess at the department's annual art show. She had hired the studio she wanted, supervised the arrangement of the art works, and dictated who would bring the food for the refreshments table. She presided over the affair with an hauteur that visibly upset several of Richard's colleagues in the department. My husband has noted with remorse that

Richard never again painted a worthy painting after
he became connected with Monica. She put him to
work making little greeting cards, painting murals on
their children's walls, and creating clever bits of sta-
tionery and envelopes for her.

*(8) Constantly manipulate and narrow the range of the in-
dividual's perceptions and feelings.* Of course this was
what Monica was doing! It is why Richard could no
longer paint with the depth and élan he had previ-
ously displayed, why he could no longer appreciate
the good times he had had with his parents and
brother, why the only things that mattered any more
were Monica and her family and their material pos-
sessions. Richard had always been almost radically in-
dividualistic and anti-materialistic. Now he appeared
to be as concerned about wealth and status as the next
person.

*(9) Make it an unswerving principle that alternative systems
must always be viewed as illegitimate, unacceptable, and
useless.* This is what had happened to our relationship.
Because it didn't conform to Monica's control and
standards, it had been overthrown and discarded.
Hers was the only acceptable way, and Richard must
conform to it or else.

*(10) Develop irrational fears in the individual about what
will happen should he or she leave or even attempt to
question authority.* Our poor son! How terrified he
must be if he even has a rebellious thought! She would
take away his palace, his financial ease, and his children—especially his children!—if he so much as questioned her decisions and manner of governing his life.

My husband is convinced this is the answer, and that Monica has stolen our son's mind and is driving it over the cliff as surely as if she were behind the wheel of an eighteen-wheeler. He may be right. We know she majored in psychology in college, but doubt if she is even conscious of the techniques she's using. It probably comes naturally to the descendant of a big business tycoon like her grandfather. She instinctively knows which buttons to push in our son's psyche to get him to be her robot for life.

Unfortunately, there's not a thing we can do about it.

We've tried. Two years ago, John wrote Richard a long letter more or less telling him that our welcome mat is always out and the latch key is on the outside. A few months later, I wrote Monica a letter, laying my heart out as a mother and grandmother. Neither of us received an answer. They've built a psychological wall between us as high and thick as the great wall of China!

From time to time, we discuss other options. Like driving by their house and watching for the children to go out to play. Like visiting little Abby and Rachel at school. Like waylaying Richard at his school. But we always conclude that there's nothing we can do if they don't want us in their lives.

It's hard. Someone in my family always forwards their Christmas card to us with the latest photo of the children on it. Now there are four of them, with the birth last year of a son. I post the photos on the refrigerator and give the children a kiss sometimes when I'm feeling melancholy. I resist the urge to tear up the photos as soon as I've seen them. That would be the easy way.

John says maybe someday one of the children will get curious and come looking for us. I'm not sure we'll live to be that old. But it's a nice thought if it comforts him.

RICHARD AS ANAKIN

For all the *Star Wars* fans, here's an interesting tidbit. Our son Eric discovered it, and brought us a copy of *Star Wars III: Revenge of the Sith* so we could see for ourselves. He had just watched the movie again, he said, and was amazed at how much his brother Richard mirrored the character of Anakin Sky-walker, the young Jedi warrior who betrays his fellow Jedis by joining the powerful Sith Emperor to take over the galaxy.

We were amazed too. Anakin looks a lot like our handsome son, and, in the beginning of the story, displays some of our son's finest qualities of strength, courage, and loyalty. But then, as he becomes seduced by dreams of power and the Emperor's whis-perings about the added strength of the Dark Side, he under-goes a metamorphosis just like Richard's.

Eventually, in the movie, Anakin fights a light-saber duel with his old Jedi master Obi-Wan Kenobi. Obi-Wan finally bests him and leaves him wounded beside an angry lake of fire. Anakin looks up from his prone position, his face distorted by passion, and growls, "I hate you!"

My husband and I looked at one another. We both remem-bered our son's distorted face in the restaurant when he told us, "I hate you and I never want to see you again!"

Obi-Wan looks at Anakin with deep regret. "You were my brother, Anakin," he said. "I loved you." We could only imagine how our son Eric felt when he watched this exchange and thought about his own brother.

The flames from the lake of fire finally engulf Anakin. But the Emperor of the Sith, sensing that his lieutenant is in danger, arrives with two attendants who carry off the charred body. They transport him to a futuristic hospital where what remains of him is resuscitated and clothed with shiny black armor, transforming him into the dark warrior known as Darth Vader, who would become the leader of the Sith in the remaining *Star Wars* episodes.

We sat there after watching the film and felt as if the breath had been knocked out of us. That was *our son* on the screen, behaving toward his closest Jedi companion the way he behaved toward us and his brother. We wouldn't have believed such a transformation in the movie had we not already experienced it in the flesh!

3

MEETING OUR PAIN-FELLOWS

I'm quite hurt; I had no idea of that much hate.

— John Updike, *Poorhouse Fair*

We are all pain-fellows.

— Christopher Fry, *A Sleep of Prisoners*

The heart that has been pierced and broken is open to receive the pain of every other heart.

— Duirmuid O'Murchu, *Catching Up With Jesus*

BEING SPURNED BY A SON you love is a profoundly painful experience.

It's almost impossible to keep yourself from thinking about him and his family. I often wake up and imagine our Richard's rising to shower and shave and get to work. Then I think of him in his classroom, where I know he is a splendid teacher. I reflect on him again in the afternoon when it is time for him to return to his family and play with the children, and sometimes in the evening as well, when I wonder what all of them are doing.

It has been long enough now that I can pretty well accept

that things are the way they are and I may never see him again. He is no longer the same person he was when we had him as a son. Looking back, I realize he began to become someone else the minute he became engaged to Monica. His face became strained and removed, as if he were living somewhere behind an invisible fence and could no longer communicate with us.

One thing I have found is that if I tell our story to another parent, there is a strong likelihood that that parent has either had a similar experience or knows someone who has. Then I hear a tale whose kinship with our own is striking, and there is a sudden recognition on both our parts that we aren't alone in our grief but that there is an almost unlimited fellowship of pain and suffering, maybe one that links millions of people in the world.

A CASUAL MEETING

One Sunday afternoon before our final split my husband and I were in Macy's shopping for an anniversary gift for Richard and Monica. We were struggling to find something we thought they would deem acceptable. Usually they didn't seem to appreciate anything we got them unless it was something they said they wanted. I remember before they were married when Monica told us to get Richard a snow blower for his birthday. We looked at them and decided they were too expensive and we wouldn't know which one to get. So we got something else. They both seemed unhappy with our gift.

But at this point, with the relationship as strained as it was, we wanted to find just the right thing.

Another couple shopping in the gift department overheard our conversation. "We have been listening to your discussion," said the wife. "Can we help you make a decision?"

We told them about our dilemma and our eagerness to get something perfect for our son and his wife.

"We'd like to find something really special," I said, "—something that will make them happy with us for a change."

That opened the floodgates. Both the man and the woman began talking about their situation with their son and his wife.

Their only son had married a few years earlier and their daughter-in-law had systematically alienated him from them. Before the wedding, they said, she had been enchanting, and they were delighted that their son was going to marry her. But everything changed once they had said, "I do."

The daughter-in-law began her campaign by refusing to go to their home for a meal. So the parents invited them to dine with them at a nice restaurant. They thought the neutral ground might appeal to her. Their son was delighted, and accepted the invitation.

But when the time came for the dinner, his wife decided not to accompany him.

Later, they learned, she told friends that her husband's parents invited him out to a meal but neglected to invite her. Apparently she repeated the lie so many times that she began to believe it herself, and one day she phoned his parents and accused them of trying to take her husband away from her.

"You expect your son to call you and come to see you and have dinner with you," she said. "Well, I have decided to put a stop to that. You are evil, selfish people. He doesn't love you. He says you are nothing but common crooks. You should hear how he talks about you when you aren't around!"

The parents had had a close, affectionate family, and wanted to share this aura of happiness with their new daughter-in-law. But the reverse had happened. Their daughter-in-law, and then their son too, let them know that they wanted nothing else to do with them. The daughter-in-law, they said, issued all kinds of ultimatums if they defied her wishes. She even threatened to kill her husband and his parents if he should ever leave her.

"It's as if she has taken over his mind," said the father. "He seems so beaten down. The last time we saw him, he had lost weight and appeared to be disoriented. He wasn't even interested in the things that he had once been crazy about."

"His eyes," said the mother, "were like stones. No expression at all. And he used to smile all the time. Now his lips are tight and straight, and he almost never smiles. Bill is right. He seems to be possessed!"

At this point the mother heaved a deep sigh. "We can't take this kind of abuse any more," she said. "We can't bear to see our son mistreated. We have lived in our house for 35 years, but we put it on the market last week."

"You mean you're going to sell out and move?" I asked.

"We're nearly 70 years old," she said, "and we can't take it any more. We have to get away from here before our health breaks. We can't bear what's happening to our son."

My husband and I commiserated with them. We felt genuinely sorry for them. They seemed so pitiful.

Afterward, I regretted not having asked for their names and address, so we could contact them and see how they were doing. At least we could have reminded them that they weren't alone.

BEN AND JOAN AND THE BORDERLINER

Two springs ago, my husband and I were vacationing in the English Lake District, probably our favorite place in all the world. We stayed at one of those cozy Bed-and-Breakfast inns where you meet everybody around the breakfast tables. We especially seemed to hit it off with a lovely couple from Alaska, Joan and Ben, and not only ate breakfast with them every day but shared a couple of dinners as well.

By the second day, they had decided to expose their heartache over their son Jeffrey, who had married the year before. Jeffrey, or Jeff, as they usually called him, was a highly successful computer programmer whose work took him all over the world. His wife Katie had also worked for the same company but had quit her job before the wedding.

Joan and Ben had heard horror stories about some of their friends' daughters-in-law, but never suspected it might become a problem with Jeff and Katie's marriage. Before the wedding, Katie had seemed nearly perfect.

"We thought she was the ideal wife for our son," said Ben.

"Our fantasy was short-lived," said Joan. "After the wedding, the reality set in. Our son had married a—well, for lack of a better word, a *witch*."

"I've called her worse," said Ben.

I thought it was interesting that he didn't laugh. I decided that he was being very serious.

"Everything changed at the wedding reception," said Joan. "Can you believe it?! They hadn't been married an hour. We were going through the reception line to congratulate them and welcome Katie into our family. But when I reached out to embrace her, she brushed my arms aside and put her hands firmly on my shoulders. 'Jeff is mine now,' she announced, 'and you are not to have anything else to do with him.'"

I was aghast. "What did you say?" I asked.

"I began to laugh. I thought it was a joke. But then I looked in her eyes and I could tell she meant it. It was no joke. She meant exactly what she had said. Jeff belonged to her now, and she wanted me to understand that. She didn't want him to have anything else to do with us."

"Just like that?"

"Just like that."

Ben shook his head solemnly in agreement.

From that moment on, said Joan, she could never do anything right around Katie. Whatever she said was misinterpreted. Katie told lies about Joan to their friends and family members, always painting her as a mother-in-law who had unnatural expectations for her son.

"It didn't do a bit of good for Joan to try to refute it," said Ben. "Katie could always top anything we said."

Joan nodded. "One evening, we were having a special dinner for some close friends, and we had invited Jeff and Katie to be there. Right in the middle of dinner, Katie announced to them, 'Jeff's mother despises me, you know. She doesn't believe any woman is good enough for her son. She knows I hate asparagus and any kind of Jell-O, but she always prepares both of them every time we eat here, just like you see tonight. She likes making me feel uncomfortable.'"

"Of course it wasn't true," said Ben. "Joan was mortified. So was I. Joan tried to laugh it off and pretend it was only a joke. But it wasn't. We could see the hate in her eyes. I think she actually wanted to destroy Joan's image in front of our friends."

"So how did you cope with this?" I asked.

Joan and Ben both shook their heads.

"What could I do?" asked Joan.

"Well," said Ben, "you remember, you invited Katie out to lunch after that to try to talk about whatever was bothering her and Jeff."

"That's right," said Joan. "I said, 'I don't know what it is exactly, but there's something terribly wrong between us. If you can tell me what it is, maybe we can work out some way to bridge our differences.'"

"And did she tell you?"

Joan moved her head slightly and looked very sad. "You know what she did? She shouted at me in a loud voice, so that everybody in the restaurant turned around to look. 'Don't you call me a bitch!' she said. 'Your foul language offends me. I'm going to repeat every word you've said to me to your son, and he will never want to see you again!'"

Joan's face showed how devastated she had been by this assault. She took out a tissue and dabbed at her eyes and nose before continuing.

Ben laid a hand on hers. Then he continued their story.

"Last year," he said, "we went to Europe for a vacation. We talked a lot about the kids and what we could do. Joan decided she needed to talk to Jeff alone, without Katie around. So when we got back home, she telephoned Jeff on his cell phone and asked if he would meet her for lunch the next day but keep it a secret from Katie. He was so excited to hear from his mother that he just burst out with, 'Mom, it's so good to hear your voice!' Apparently Katie was in the room with him. The minute he finished that sentence, Joan could hear Katie in the background screaming at him to hang up the phone. She reminded him she had forbidden him to have any contact with us and that he had promised he wouldn't."

My husband waited a second, then asked, "So what happened?"

Joan replied, "We didn't have lunch. And sometime later we learned that Katie had been so angry that she had hit his dog on the head with a big wooden spoon with enough force to break it in half."

At this point, Joan openly burst into tears and cried for a

minute or two before we continued the conversation. Ben was sniffling too.

"I could write volumes about that woman," Joan said at last, mopping the tears from her face and blowing her nose, "and all the lies she substitutes for reality."

She gulped and sighed.

"I might as well tell you the rest," she said, looking over at Ben, then back at us. "A psychiatrist told Jeff that Katie has something called Borderline Personality Disorder."

We were familiar with the term, but listened patiently as Joan explicated it for us.

"Borderliners, as they're called," she said, "are people who never bonded properly with their mothers. They learn to fabricate new personalities for themselves from the time they're very young. Maybe even when they're still in the crib. So by the time they're six or seven, they're very artful liars. You can't ever believe anything they say."

"They're very hard to deal with," contributed Ben, "even for psychiatrists. This fellow told Jeff that they usually outsmart their shrinks."

"They're often homosexuals," added Joan.

"And alcoholics or drug addicts," said Ben.

"I was getting to that," she said. "Jeff says Katie drinks anything that has alcohol in it. One night she got up while Jeff was sleeping and drank a whole bottle of furniture polish, and he had to rush her to the ER. Afterward, she insisted she hadn't done it, but Jeff found the empty bottle and knew she had."

"After Jeff told us about it," said Ben, "we found a book about borderline personality disorder. It was called *I Hate You, Don't Leave Me.*" He fished in his billfold and came out with a crumpled piece of paper and unfolded it. "I copied out the main characteristics," he said, holding the paper toward us. "It listed most of the things Joan mentioned, plus a couple of others. One of them was 'frequent and inappropriate displays of anger.'"

When Ben said this, I thought of our own son and his wife, and wondered if they could both be borderliners.

"We don't know what to do for Jeff," said Joan, resignedly. "That woman has him trapped. He isn't himself any more. He stutters a lot now."

"This isn't how it's supposed to be," added Ben.

We agreed. Jeff had got himself into a terrible situation, and by getting into it himself, he had got his folks into it too.

We exchanged Christmas cards with Joan and Ben for a couple of years, then didn't contact one another any more. But we often wonder about Jeff and Katie and what has happened in their marriage.

I ought to write Joan again and ask how they're doing.

DAVE AND PATTI AND THE CHRISTMAS VISIT

Our neighbors Dave and Patti were eagerly awaiting a brief visit from their son Bob and his wife Betsy. It was going to be a very brief visit, because Bob and Betsy's sole mission was to bring their dog to board with Bob's parents while they proceeded to another state to spend Christmas with Betsy's parents and other relatives.

Dave and Patti were used to slim pickings with their son since he married Patti. So they actually looked forward to at least a brief visit, with a hug and a kiss, before sending him and Betsy on their way. The dog, an Airedale named Sandy, was a delight and they were looking forward, if they couldn't have Christmas with their son, to spoiling his dog.

By mid-morning, though, it had begun snowing very hard,

and the snow was predicted to last through the evening. In the late afternoon, therefore, when Bob and Betsy and Sandy reached the turn-off to Bob's parents' home, Betsy made the unilateral decision that they shouldn't delay by going by the parents' home to leave the dog because they might get snowed in and not make it to her parents' house.

"But we have to leave Sandy with my folks," Bob said. "Your parents don't have room for him."

It was true. They lived in a small, shotgun-style house and space was at a premium when their two children arrived with their families for the holidays.

"I'm sorry," said Betsy, "but it's snowing hard now and I don't want to take a chance on not getting home. I don't want to be stuck with your parents on Christmas day. We're not stopping."

Bob, according to the story as we later heard it, kept driving because he knew that once Betsy's mind was made up there was no altering it. He didn't even stop to telephone his parents about the change of plans until they reached his in-laws' house. He was truly sorry, he said, and promised to stop and see them on New Year's Eve as they drove home.

Dave and Patti were disappointed but tried to keep their negative thoughts to themselves. This sort of thing had often happened before, and they always believed in the motto "least said, soonest mended."

"To be perfectly truthful," Patti confided to us, "it was becoming a stressful meeting every time we were together."

When Betsy and Bob concluded their Christmas visit with her folks and started their trip home, Betsy announced that she needed to get back early to rest up before returning to work after New Year's and that therefore they shouldn't go by Bob's parents' house at all. She issued one of her ultimatums, ordering

Bob to keep driving until they reached home.

Bob had had enough, however. He wanted to see his parents and so, on one of his rare occasions, defied Betsy. He exited off the interstate highway onto the state road leading to his parents' house.

An ominous silence filled the car.

When they heard the car in the driveway, Dave and Patti flung open the front door and waited with outstretched arms to greet the children. Brushing past them without speaking, Betsy marched upstairs and sequestered herself in the guest bedroom until dinner was announced a few hours later. Then she came to the table without saying a word and remained sullenly silent throughout the meal.

Dave and Patti, after several dismal attempts at trying to include her in the conversation, finally quit making the attempt and concentrated their attention on Bob, who was happy to be with them and was very talkative. They all assumed Betsy would come around in time.

After dinner, she went back upstairs and wasn't seen again until breakfast, when, once more, she gave them all the silent treatment.

The only time she ever became animated, said Patti in recalling the visit, was when her cell phone rang. Then she would suddenly become upbeat and cheerful while talking to her boss or a friend on the line. But the minute the call was over and she put her phone away, she instantly reverted to stony silence.

This behavior went on for a couple of days, and Bob and his parents were miserable. Bob couldn't explain his wife's behavior. When Patti mentioned it in a questioning way, Bob simply shrugged his shoulders. She and Dave knew he was ashamed of the way she was acting, so they didn't press him.

Dave remembered that Betsy had loved a special Amish gift

shop in their town, so he suggested that they all go shopping for after-Christmas specials. Betsy perked up at once, and he and Patti hoped that they had all turned a corner and things would be better. They bundled up and started out to the garage, when Betsy suddenly addressed her husband for the first time in three days.

"Where is the package Mom and Dad asked me to mail?" she demanded.

"Dad and I took it to the post office yesterday," Bob said innocently.

"That's all it took," said Patti in telling the story. "She began screaming and berating Bob for mailing that damned package. That was *hers* to do, she said, not his, and he was never to touch her things. Bob was flabbergasted and tried to apologize, but she just kept haranguing him."

"It was like she was demon-possessed," added Dave.

But Patti had had enough. This particular outburst tipped the scales for her, and she lit into Betsy.

"You shut your mouth, young woman," she ordered, "and go back upstairs to your room and stay there! You are a spoiled brat, and I don't ever want you to come to our home again until you have learned how to behave like an adult. This kind of behavior is totally unacceptable in this house."

Dave said he expected Betsy to lash back at Patti, maybe even strike her. But she turned and disappeared up the stairs and remained there until dinner, when Dave took them all out to a restaurant to avoid having to sit at their own table with her. They left for home the next morning.

Betsy marched silently to their van as Bob said goodbye to his parents. They hugged him extra tight, patted his back, and whispered assurances to him, then watched the van pull away and felt heavy of heart for what they knew their son was going to endure on the ride home.

They reported to us that they never saw Betsy again.

Bob later told them that she gave him the silent treatment all the way home and kept it up for several days after they arrived. When she did begin to communicate again, her temper was so harsh and violent that he said he was physically afraid of her. Terrified of what she might do, he slept with his clothes on so he could make a quick getaway if necessary.

After a few more months of this living hell, Bob mustered the courage to file for a divorce. The day the papers were served, he moved out of their apartment and into a small one of his own, taking only the things he would need for a short stay. This turned out to be a mistake, as Betsy had the locks changed and also threw away a lot of his clothes before he finally got a court order and was able to retrieve what was left.

Patti told me it took him several months to begin to put his life back together again without that vicious woman terrorizing him. But eventually he began to feel calm and self-possessed again. And once the divorce was finalized, he took a job in another state, wanting to put as much distance as possible between himself and the woman he called "the wife from hell."

"Thank God," said Patti, "he walks with a spring in his step again!"

THE TICKLISH PROBLEM

I'm not stupid. I know there are parents-in-law from hell too. Not all of us are doting, loving parents of sons. And not all daughters-in-law are toxic like the ones I've been describing. I have friends whose daughters-in-law are loving, thoughtful, and wonderfully wholesome—all the things I wanted for our own son Richard.

But there seem to be a lot more of these mean-spirited, to-tally-selfish women out there now than there ever were in the past. Now that we've been made aware of the problem by our experience with Monica, we seem to see it on every hand—in church, in the supermarket, in stores, at the gym. I overhear some of these narcissistic women talking about their hus-bands—what bums they are, how stupid they are, how they're good for nothing but providing a monthly paycheck or carrying out the garbage—and it's all I can do to resist the desire to choke them.

Somehow, I blame the feminist revolution for a lot of it. Not in principle. In principle, it was high time women got equal treatment with men—equal pay, equal respect, equal opportu-nities. But I think the heady climate of women's rights, as it began to dominate the classroom and the workplace, empow-ered a lot of selfish, nasty females to see the world as their oyster and men as the exploitable factotums to get them what they wanted. In a PC world, they began to realize that they had an edge over the men around them that not only protected them from abuse but gave them a kind of ticket to abuse the men with impunity.

In my parents' world, men were clearly dominant. My mother sometimes got boiling mad at my father, but had no re-course but to do whatever he told her. Now that the power has begun to flow in the opposite direction, a lot of women, espe-cially in the younger generation, feel entitled to behave as self-ishly and despotically as they like, and know they won't have to pay a price for it. They can seem coquettish and desirable around men until they have them on a leash, then treat them as cruelly and insensitively as they like.

The parents I've talked with about this—those whose sons

are married to such women—are at their wits' ends.

"What can we do?" they plead. "Why does our daughter-in-law have the power to reduce our family to turmoil? Don't we praise her enough, and make her feel comfortable with our family? What did she expect when she married our son? Why does she regard us as her mortal enemies? Is there anything we can do to placate her and turn this failed situation around?"

I think about Monica, our daughter-in-law, and how hard we tried to be good to her and win her over. We always spoke sweetly to her. I praised her for how she looked or what she was wearing. I cooked things I knew she liked. My husband and I both tried to avoid talking about any subject that might be in the least bit incendiary. We really walked on eggshells just to keep her happy. My e-mails to her were filled with compliments, upbeat remarks, and attempts to stroke her ego. As I reflect on it, I realize that I practically became a nonperson in the effort to keep her happy and make myself acceptable to her. And it never worked!

The parents of sons I mention in this book are all the same. They have deep frown lines etched in their faces. They chew their lips and move their hands a lot. They look sad and worried. They confess that they're hurt and bewildered, and have done everything they know to do to try to make peace in the family, only to be rebuffed by haughty, uncaring daughters-in-law, and then, as often as not, by their sons too.

I often think of a little jingle I first heard from my mother years ago, when I was a child. "A son is a son till he gets a wife," she would say, "a daughter's a daughter the rest of her life." It's an old saying—so old that there seems to be no record of where it originated—which only proves that it isn't a new problem. But it is so often true that it's almost axiomatic.

I look at my friends who had daughters and envy them.

I wish I could hold all the parents of sons in my arms and assure them that everything will work out in the end, but I can't. We've been dealing with it in Richard and Monica now for seven years, and I can't see any light at the end of our particular tunnel. Like the nursery rhyme about Humpty-Dumpty, I'm afraid it's all over. Our relationship with Richard has fallen off the wall and there isn't any way to salvage it.

As I said in the beginning, this book doesn't really offer a cure for the problem. The only gift I can offer is one of awareness. I believe it helps all of us who have to deal with irredeemable daughters-in-law to know that we aren't alone with our own situations, that there are thousands, probably millions, of other parents out there who are as baffled and hurt as we are.

Later, I'll suggest some practical ways of dealing with these terrible situations. But for now it's important to hear some more stories and realize more deeply and clearly what a widespread problem it is.

4

THE TRAGEDY OF MISSED BIRTHDAYS AND HOLIDAYS

> GEORGE: You can sit there in that chair of yours, you can sit there with the gin running out of your mouth, and you can humiliate me, you can tear me apart...ALL NIGHT... And that's perfectly all right... that's OK...
> MARTHA: YOU CAN STAND IT!
> GEORGE: I CANNOT STAND IT!
> MARTHA: YOU CAN STAND IT! YOU MARRIED ME FOR IT!
>
> —— Edward Albee, *Who's Afraid of Virginia Woolf?*

> The number of injuries a typical man has endured is astounding.
>
> —— Robert Bly, *Iron John*

> My life in those days seemed to be a succession of disasters.
>
> —— Hugh Leonard, *Home Before Night*

PAULO SAID, "I WISH I had never married Maggie."
"Amen," his parents Don and Isabella replied in unison.

We have known Paulo and his family for 35 years. His parents are good, solid people. He and his four siblings grew up in a home filled with love, laughter, fun, and music. Everybody in the community loved Paulo, who was known for his beautiful voice. He was constantly asked to sing at various functions. The rest of his family played musical instruments and sang as well.

They had their own band and vocal group that often entertained in clubs and churches in the area.

All four of the children matured into wholesome, happy adults. They were full of life, and life seemed to agree with them.

Paulo met Maggie his senior year in college. She seemed lovely, pleasant, and courteous. He was shy around girls, but eventually got up the courage to ask her for a date. It wasn't long before they were going steady.

When Paulo decided Maggie was the woman he wanted to marry, he brought her home to meet his parents. They were delighted with her. Like Paulo, she loved music, art, theater, museums, and reading. Every member of the family hoped she would marry Paulo. It couldn't get any better, they said.

As time went by, though, Paulo and his parents discovered another side—a wholly unexpected side—to Maggie's personality that disturbed them. The more secure she became in Paulo's love, the bossier and more controlling she became. When she told Paulo to jump, she expected him to say "How high?" She began imposing her decisions on him about everything, even down to the kind of designer clothes she thought he ought to wear.

Don and Isabella were worried about the girl's overpowering personality, but thought Paulo would surely be strong enough to produce some adjustments in her. "NOP," they said to one another—not our problem."

Sadly, though, it became their problem.

As Don and Isabella learned more about Maggie, they realized she was raised in a home very unlike their own. Her parents were irritable, overbearing people. They seldom gave Maggie any signs of love or approbation. Paulo was the first to comment on this.

"I felt," he said after meeting them for the first time, "as if I had walked into a pit of vipers."

He had driven Maggie home in an old car his grandmother had given him when she no longer needed it. It did look somewhat disreputable, but so did a lot of other students' cars, and Paulo loved it.

When Maggie's dad saw the car, he made fun of it and told Paulo never to park it in front of his house again. "If you have to drive that bucket of bolts," he said, "leave it around the corner so nobody will think it belongs to us."

"When I heard this," said Isabella, "I thought of the British comedy *Keeping Up Appearances*. "You know, the one where Hyacinth Bucket always tries to make her brother-in-law Onslow keep his old rattletrap of a car away from her house."

It didn't bother Paulo that Maggie's dad didn't like his car, but it did bother him that her parents could be cruel to their only child. He thought it unnatural that they should treat her so disrespectfully all the time, and, what is more, that they should indicate that he could expect to receive the same kind of treatment if he became their son-in-law. Paulo felt very sorry for Maggie and wanted to protect her. Instead of making him wary of marrying her, her parents' meanness and disregard only strengthened his determination to marry her and rescue her from the home she had grown up in.

With all the baggage from her own home life, Maggie gave the impression that she truly liked Paulo's parents. She seemed to feel very comfortable around them, and apparently felt more or less adopted by them. One day she brought them a warm loaf of bread she had just baked. They all sat around the table, sliced it, slathered some butter and jam on it, and ate it with milk and tea.

When Maggie excused herself to go to the bathroom, Paulo

told his parents that Maggie's mother had been irate about her making the bread for them. "She said Maggie had to pay for every bit of the ingredients because she didn't intend to spend money feeding my family."

After that, Don and Isabella also wanted to claim Maggie for their own and get her away from such cruel, unpleasant parents.

Paulo felt trapped. He liked Maggie and wanted to marry her, but he was afraid of being drawn into the spider's web of her family, so he kept putting off buying an engagement ring.

She, on the other hand, had determined that they should get married, and eventually she cajoled Paulo into it.

Before Paulo came on the scene, she had been dating a well-established young lawyer. This had greatly pleased her parents, for they could see themselves profiting from the marriage. In fact, they openly alluded to their being set up for life.

"Maggie owes us, and Ken can pay us back," they said.

But when Maggie announced that she was going to marry Paulo, they became extremely upset. "Why the devil would you consider marryin' a fool like him?" demanded her father. "He hasn't got a penny to his name. Look at that old car he drives."

"I love him," she said, "and he treats me like a queen."

At this, her father let loose a string of oaths and announced. "If you marry that fool, I'll not pay for the wedding!"

He kept the promise, and Maggie and Paulo took out a loan to pay for the extravagant affair she wanted.

It was the beginning of their financial downfall.

Both Paulo and his parents believed that, once he and Maggie were married, they could love her into forgetting her past. A little TLC, they thought, would be just the ticket. So they all went overboard trying to please her.

No matter what they did for her or how much they loved

her, though, it proved too little to cancel out the years of negativity she had experienced with her parents. What they didn't realize was that a part of Maggie herself had absorbed the angry, hateful behavior of her parents and had learned to react to everything the same way they did.

It didn't take long for them to discover that Maggie was a complex, anguished, mentally ill person who would never escape from the ways of her parents.

She totally dominated Paulo.

He didn't offer much resistance, as it always seemed easier to go along with her than to argue with her, which made her very unhappy. Whenever he questioned her actions or opinions—on rare occasions—she accused him of being like her parents and making her say or do bad things. Sometimes she berated him for hours on end. Then she would exhibit remorse and cry copious tears because she felt so guilt-ridden. The waterworks might end abruptly and suddenly she would place all the blame on Paulo again. It was almost a carbon copy of the way she had been treated by her parents.

Paulo desperately looked for ways to defuse her anger. Sometimes he would take her to fancy restaurants beyond their means. Even then, she would often become inexplicably angry as they were eating and curse Paulo, the waiter, the manager, and occasionally even guests at nearby tables. He took her shopping at expensive boutiques. There, she might well lose her temper with a clerk and demand that Paulo tell off the clerk in no uncertain terms, or she would do it herself and flounce out of the store like some temperamental diva.

Her shopping sprees became legendary in the family. If she saw a pair of shoes she liked, she not only bought them, regardless of how costly, but might buy the same pair in every color the store had. If she fancied a designer blouse, she would ask for half a dozen. Money flowed through her hands like water. She soon maxed out every credit card she and Paulo could get.

As their debt grew, so did their secrecy. Paulo later told his parents that Maggie wanted it that way. She said their spending was nobody's business but theirs, and that she didn't want him to tell his parents anything. But Don and Isabella noticed that the few visits they now had from them seemed always to coincide with a time when they were particularly strapped for cash.

"They need money again," Don began to say whenever he saw them walking toward the front door. He was never wrong.

One day Isabella said, "Don, we can't give them any more money. It isn't helping them to face their responsibilities. We don't know how much they owe, and they don't tell us anything. They just come with their hands out. I think they're on a roller-coaster ride into debt with no real thought about the consequences."

Isabella didn't realize it at the time, but her observation was dead-on. The very next day, Paulo and Maggie signed for a new house on the other side of town.

"I wonder where they got the loan," said Don when he heard it. But he knew better than to ask. Maggie had drilled Paulo well about secrecy, and he never told them anything any more. Not even the address of their new house or the new phone number they got when they moved in.

Don and Isabella no longer even knew how to contact them.

A PERSONAL MUSING

When our friends were telling us this story, I thought to myself, "It follows the pattern I'm beginning to recognize in all cases of estranged sons and their wives. It's almost as if the son and his wife are 'murdering' his family, or at least getting rid of them, by imposing a code of silence and never letting them in on anything again."

How long can a son raised in a nice home continue to give his parents the cold shoulder that way? What happens to all the old family ties and loyalties? Does the son ever feel really guilty about severing the relationship? Can he forget how good they've been to him through the years and how much he actually owes them? How can he turn his back on people who have loved and cared for him so faithfully for so many years?

There is probably nothing in all the son's years at home that prepares his parents for the hurt and betrayal they feel when he marries and his wife decrees that he is not to have anything else to do with them, that he is not to tell them anything, that he is not to contact them, that he is to go on with his life as if his parents were already deceased. They have never known anything but love for him, and then he deserts them as if they were hideous people he had just been waiting to get away from. They can't begin to comprehend such a change. They feel as if some vital, intimate part of their lives has been surgically removed—without an anesthetic!

Don and Isabella said they thought they would go crazy. Sometimes Don became so angry with Paulo for what he and Maggie were doing to his mother that he wanted to find out where their house was, go over there with an ax, chop down the front door, and threaten both of them with dismemberment for their heinous crimes against the family. Other times he said he wanted to sit and cry because of the way their lives had fallen apart.

"Nothing really matters any more," he said in a very sad voice. "Life isn't the same without our son."

THE CONTINUING STORY

Year after year, Paulo and Maggie remained in desperate need of money. Paulo had a good job, but he spent most of his time at work worrying about how he was going to pay the credit bills Maggie kept racking up. Their house payment was past due almost every month. Their phone and utility services were frequently discontinued. Their life insurance lapsed. If Paulo's health insurance hadn't been through his company, they wouldn't have had that. Twice, the bank threatened to foreclose on their house.

Maggie, meanwhile, never flagged. Even while all these dominoes were cascading, she continued to want the best things money or credit could buy. It was almost like a sport to her to see how high she could run up a credit line before it was cut off. And if Paulo attempted to chide or correct her, she launched into a tirade against him and his family for not being wealthy. She especially liked to remind him of the lawyer she might have married.

"He would have given me anything I want," she once said with a sigh.

During the period while Paulo and Maggie were out of contact with Don and Isabella, Maggie's parents died within a few months of one another. She inherited some money from the sale of their house, and she and Paulo used it to reduce a lot of their credit bills. But nothing seemed to change her increasingly demonic personality. She continued to spend, throw frequent tantrums, and exhibit pathological anger toward Paulo's parents.

"Why don't they take out a second mortgage on their house?" she would scream at him. "They could help us if they would. They are the most selfish people I ever saw!"

She never seemed to recognize the irony in speaking this way of people with whom she allowed no communication whatsoever.

As his parents would later learn, Paulo became very depressed. After years of spousal abuse, he could no longer even think straight. He felt desperately alone because he had alienated his parents, who always loved him, for this woman who did nothing but spend money and harangue him for not being rich. And he was exhausted from trying to cope with the bills, bills, bills, and the continual threats from credit agencies. Often, he later told his parents, there wasn't even enough money in the house to go to the grocery and buy food.

On top of all this, Maggie would occasionally overdose on pills in what appeared to be a fake suicide attempt. Paulo would never know if she was merely using this method of ratcheting down his growing frustration with her or if she really wanted to end it all.

At last, when everything seemed overwhelming to him, Paulo went to a lawyer friend who encouraged him to file for bankruptcy. He decided it was the only thing he could do. Maggie was outraged by the idea because she thought it was demeaning. "If you do such a stupid thing," she told him, "I'll leave you and take everything!"

"There isn't anything to take except unpaid bills, Maggie," he said. "Our debts are all we have left." If he hadn't been so beaten, he might have smiled as he said this. But he didn't.

That night, they fought for hours.

In the end, she was in tears and he was exhausted from all the abuse she had heaped on him. In the wee hours of the morning, they agreed to separate. Paulo would stay in the house and she would move to an apartment. The arrangement would give them a chance to cool off and make some long-range decisions about their future.

Unfortunately, Maggie didn't let Paulo off that easily.

Often, when he came home from work, she would be waiting on the front porch to demand some money. When he told her there wasn't any, she would go ballistic and threaten to take him to court. She was totally irrational about everything.

After a few months of this, Paulo made up his mind. He filed for divorce and proceeded to take bankruptcy. He sold their house, but they were so far behind on payments that he had to borrow money to close the deal.

None of this appeared to affect Maggie. She went on spending as if there were no tomorrow.

Alone most of the time now, Paulo began to reflect on his life, and what a shell of a person he had become during all those years with Maggie. He went to work every day, did his job without communicating with others, then came home and sequestered himself in an apartment. He didn't trust anyone.

Don and Isabella tried repeatedly to see him. They left countless invitations for him to come home for a visit or a meal. But he didn't want to see them or be with them. He lost his appetite, and sometimes couldn't even remember if he had eaten. He wasn't even interested in music, which had once been his very life. He began to suffer panic attacks.

There was only one thing he was sure of. He didn't want Maggie back.

A SUDDEN TURN OF EVENTS

Then, a few months after the divorce, Paulo received the most stunning news he had ever had. Maggie had been found dead in her apartment. The police said she had overdosed on prescription drugs.

Before, when she had tried to end her life, Paulo had always found her and got her to the ER in time. Now, alone, she had managed to carry it off. Her demons had finally been satisfied.

At first, Paulo turned to his parents. They helped him through the funeral arrangements, the service, and the burial. But he was eaten up with guilt, and they were unable to get through to him about this. Soon he stopped seeing them at all. He dropped out of church and cancelled the few singing invitations he had been fulfilling. He didn't return phone calls or e-mails.

Don and Isabella felt helpless. Paulo had frozen them out of his life again, and they were beside themselves with anguish and concern.

But something unexpected happened that shocked Paulo back into the land of the living.

Part of his therapy, as he tried to get over Maggie's death, was a daily bike ride after work. One afternoon, as he rode along on a busy highway, a car turned the wrong way and he collided with it. He was hurled through the car's windshield and suffered multiple lacerations and broken bones.

Hospitalized for days, he had a lot of time to reflect on everything.

His parents and brothers visited him regularly. One day he told Don and Isabella that there were ways in which he was like Maggie.

"I'm afraid of everything," he said. "I'm not talking about a normal, short-term fear like being afraid of another wreck. I'm scared to death of everything. Maggie was that way. If she coughed, she knew she had TB. If she found a lump on her arm, she knew it was cancer. When we boarded a plane, she knew it would crash. My fears are as crazy and unreasonable as hers.

"I keep everything to myself, the way she did. You know, like when you say to me that I hold things close to my vest. I don't want anyone to know my inner thoughts. I'm a loner, but I bemoan the fact that I don't have friends. I'm really mixed up!

"Luckily," he added, "I don't have violent outbursts the way Maggie did. I only want to be quiet and hide from things, to pull the covers over my head."

His parents weren't sure if Paulo was confessing these things because of his medications or if he was simply facing the truth about himself and wanted to get some things off his chest. But they were happy to hear him talking to them so intimately, and hoped the long, difficult years of separation and loneliness were finally coming to an end. Perhaps he was going to be their son again, and they could all begin to heal together.

Things haven't been perfect for them. Paulo has seldom spoken so openly since that occasion in the hospital, and still keeps a shield of privacy around his affairs. But he has returned to church with new zest and has taken on a lot of new singing opportunities. He returns his parents' calls and e-mails—most of the time—and comes by their house for Thanksgiving and Christmas and birthdays and other special occasions.

Except for some deep scarring, says Isabella, he seems to have come through his ordeal reasonably well.

"We don't know how he feels about all those lost years," she says. "But his dad and I can't help grieving about them. They were horrible for all of us."

Don agrees.

"I love to see him when he comes by," he adds, "and I always manage to put an arm around him and try to reassure him that things are going to be okay. But I feel sad about it all. Think of all the birthdays and holidays we missed spending together. You can't ever get those back. They're gone forever!"

5

MEANWHILE, IN A PARALLEL UNIVERSE

In the beginning is relation.

— Martin Buber, *I and Thou*

I am the poet of the woman the same as
the man,
And I say it is as great to be a woman as
to be a man,
And I say there is nothing greater than
the mother of men.

— Walt Whitman, *Song of Myself*

Everything is different since it changed.

— Doris Grumbach, in Frank Conroy,
ed., *The Eleventh Draft*

IN THIS CHAPTER, I AM really going out on a limb. So far, I have been writing about heterosexual marriages in which the male so totally submits to the female that he neglects his original family or is even estranged from them. But now I want to consider whether the same phenomenon I have been describing doesn't also exist in partnerships in same-gender relationships.

My husband and I have known hundreds of gay men and lesbian couples through our work with various churches. Many of them are or have been close friends of ours. And I believe, from my observations, that some gay men and lesbians have the same problems with parents as the heterosexual couples I've been discussing. One of the partners—usually the more "feminine" of the two—can be just as disruptive of his or her partner's relationships with parents as Monica or Katie or Betsy or Maggie or any other woman in this book.

The same-gender relationship situation being what it is, there are often ruptures in relationships with parents even before there is a partner to have problems with. Many parents, once they learn their child is a gay man or lesbian, lack the grace and understanding to embrace the child and move on. So in their case the matter of a partner's acceptance of the parents becomes moot.

But among others—in situations where parents are understanding and accept the fact that their children are gay men or lesbians—there are often cases in which the "feminine" partner does "her" best to block the "masculine" partner's relationship with "his" parents.

EDITH AND DOROTHY

Take the story of Edith and Dorothy, for example—two lesbians we knew through their parents, who were close friends of ours.

Edith and Dorothy had been next-door neighbors since birth, and started to kindergarten together. Both their fathers and Dorothy's mother were employed by the state university in their community, so it wasn't a surprise that the girls attended the K-12 school attached to the university and remained close friends through all those years.

Edith, our friends' daughter, was a fair, curly-headed doll with the face of an angel. Her parents weren't wealthy, but they were well-to-do and gave her everything she could want. It was a treat for her classmates to be invited to play at her house after school, because she had a playroom crammed with wonderful toys, including a table set for a tea party with four frilly-dressed dolls sitting in wicker chairs around it. There was also a big TV set in the room with shelf after shelf of children's videos surrounding it. And at one end of the room there was a big closet holding a wealth of old evening clothes, boxes of costume jewelry, big hats, and high-heeled shoes for playing dress-up. Edith and her little friends made up skits, donned the colorful outfits, and entertained themselves for hours at a time.

On her birthday, her mother always hosted a magical party for her entire class at school. There were several tubs of ice cream in different flavors and a huge, beautifully decorated cake. The children who were lucky enough to get a slice of cake with a candle on it received a special prize, and every child received such favors as coloring books, boxes of crayons, and paddle balls. Edith's mother brought lively games to play, and often told enchanting stories. Those birthday parties were treasured by everyone in Edith's class.

Her childhood years were a dream. In the summer she vacationed with her parents and siblings at a beach or they all traveled overseas. As president of the university, her father had access to apartments in various European universities, and he and his family took advantage of these accommodations to experience as many countries as possible. From the time she was six, they often took Edith's friend Dorothy with them.

Edith dated a little in high school, primarily in order to attend the various dances sponsored by school organizations. But she didn't find the boys very exciting. Secretly, she was content not to have a steady boyfriend the way many girls did. She also dated a few times in college, but preferred the boys who were happy-go-lucky and weren't always trying to get her to commit to a permanent relationship.

After college, she spent a lot of time with a young math professor in her father's university named Matthew Moore. Matthew was intelligent, respected in the academic community, and the right age. He was also very handsome. Edith's parents liked him and encouraged her to take his courtship seriously. She tried to do so for their sakes, as she felt that they had done a lot for her and she owed them that much.

"I can't let them down," she said to Dorothy.

After more than three years of dating, Matthew was eager to give Edith a ring and secure her promise to marry him. "I love you and your family," he said. "Why can't you make a commitment to me? Is there something wrong with me?"

Edith told him that of course there wasn't, it was just that she always had a difficult time making decisions of a permanent kind and marriage seemed so final. "What I really meant to say," she continued, "is that marriage is for a lifetime, and I don't want to take my vows lightly."

Matthew pled that they had been going together for a long time and it was now time for them to come to a more permanent arrangement or else give up the relationship altogether. Edith could tell by the set of his jaw and the look in his eyes that this was not an idle threat. She asked him to give her a few more days before she made the decision.

HER CLOSEST FRIEND

Dorothy, Edith's best friend and long-time confidante, was in many ways Edith's opposite. As a child, she had been a dark-headed, brown-eyed tomboy. There probably wasn't a tree in the whole neighborhood to whose top she hadn't climbed. She was always banging herself up in some physical activity. Her mother often said, "I didn't know what her knees looked like until she was sixteen."

Dorothy was a terror on the basketball court and loved to play football with her brother and his friends. She could hit a baseball farther than most of the boys with whom she played. When she played tennis, her opponents knew to duck when she hit a ball in their direction.

Dorothy's father was an assistant dean at the university and then became the dean. Her mother was employed in the library. They encouraged their three children to read, listen to classical music, appreciate art, learn foreign languages, and develop their imaginations. Like Edith's family, they often traveled to Europe and stayed in lodgings available through European universities.

Dorothy tried to accommodate her parents' notion of how she should behave. She was only a passable student, though, because she was more interested in sports than books. When she graduated from high school, she received numerous offers of scholarships to play tennis, volleyball, basketball, and lacrosse. Because she didn't want to leave Edith, she accepted a tennis scholarship from the university where their parents worked.

She got along well with everyone. Even though she seldom dated, she had a lot of boy friends. If her parents ever chided her for seeming to discourage any permanent relationships, she merely joked, "Nobody wants to date a girl in an athletic bra and tennis shoes."

After graduation she took a position teaching physical education in a nearby high school, while continuing to live at home.

One evening at dinner, her mother told her she'd heard that Edith and Matt were getting married in June, barely three months away.

Dorothy was amazed. "Why didn't she mention it?" she asked. "I saw her only two days ago, and she didn't breathe a word."

Dorothy knew Edith and Matt had been a couple for years, but didn't think they would ever marry. Somehow, in a strange way she wouldn't mention to anyone, she always felt that Edith belonged to her. She was so delicate and helpless, and Dorothy had been her protector. But if she was getting married—well, their relationship would have to be different. Matt would be her caretaker from then on.

The wedding took place, and Matt and Edith honeymooned in Hawaii. Outwardly, they gave every appearance of being happy. Everybody expected them to start a family right away. But Edith wasn't really happy. She later confessed that she couldn't understand it, because Matt was always kind and thoughtful. Yet it was a kind of struggle for her to be his wife, and that made her feel guilty.

A year or so later, Dorothy became acutely aware of the loneliness she had felt since Edith married. They still saw one another, and Dorothy often had dinner with her and Matt. But there was something missing in her life. She decided she wanted to become a minister, and enrolled in a seminary on the West Coast. After graduation, she became pastor of a medium-sized church in the Midwest, where she worked hard and was very successful. Everybody in her parish liked her, and they called her Sister Dorothy, an appellation she enjoyed as warm and affirming.

One Sunday without warning, Dorothy looked out from her pulpit and saw Edith and Matt in the congregation, only two rows from the front. They had chosen not to tell her they'd be there because they wanted to surprise her. It was a huge surprise. Dorothy was so flabbergasted that she spent most of her time for the announcements greeting them and then forgot to give the announcements. After church, they went to lunch and spent the afternoon together.

Despite the girls' happiness at seeing one another, there was a negative side to their meeting. Edith, who had always been so meek and mild, was being supercritical of Matt. He couldn't seem to do anything to please her. Dorothy actually felt sorry for him. But Edith was plainly tired of being married to Matt, and didn't mince any words about it, even in front of him. Before the afternoon was over, she asked him to go on to the business assignment that had brought them Dorothy's way and let her spend a few days with Dorothy.

Matt agreed. Under the circumstances, he didn't seem at all sorry to do it.

Both women had more fun than they had had in years. They told stories, recalled old times together, laughed, sat up late watching movies, went hiking in the nearby mountains, and even—at Dorothy's insistence—went parasailing over a lake.

By the time Matt returned to collect Edith, the two women knew they never wanted to be separated again. They had spoken openly of their deep affection for one another, and of the strange feelings evoked by being in one another's arms. They realized they wanted to be partners for the rest of their lives. Edith told Matt she wanted a divorce, and he agreed not to contest it.

A few weeks later, the two women planned a gathering of their two families at a ski resort the families had visited together several years before. They wanted to share their news in a place all of them loved. Afterward, they realized that the ski resort was a mistake. They hadn't fully anticipated what a shock their announcement would be to their families, and when it came, they were in such close quarters that it was impossible to get away from one another to think and absorb what had transpired.

"Give us time," Edith's father said. "Look at how long it has taken the two of you to make this commitment. We need to get used to the idea. You can't expect us to get our heads around it in a weekend."

"We still love you," Dorothy's dad said, his voice trembling. "Just the way we always did. But don't be hard on us if we can't quite see our way yet to celebrating this decision with you."

The mothers cried a lot.

The siblings were more resilient, and went from shock to acceptance rather quickly, which helped Edith and Dorothy a lot.

Although both sets of parents had a difficult time accepting the partnership, it was Dorothy's parents that Edith blamed for not embracing it more eagerly. She decided she didn't like Dorothy's parents, and, for that matter, one of Dorothy's brothers, who didn't seem to be as supportive as the other siblings. Before they left the ski resort to return home, Edith let Dorothy know that she did not look forward to sharing her with them any more.

From that weekend on, Edith registered displeasure if Dorothy even telephoned her parents to check on them. She also began to resent Dorothy's buying gifts for her family, especially her mother, and the resentment grew progressively worse. She started openly resisting visits from Dorothy's parents, and soon began finding reasons not to visit them.

When Dorothy suggested a few months later that the two families plan another vacation together, Edith threatened to leave her if she arranged such a tryst. When Dorothy demanded to know why Edith felt so strongly about it, Edith said she just did, and that was that. She said she got bad "vibes" from Edith's mother.

As a consequence, the relationship between Dorothy and her parents became so strained that they wondered if it wasn't Dorothy who was willing the estrangement. They thought it would be easier for their daughter if they simply bowed out of her life. But they decided to make one last attempt at salvaging the relationship before writing it off. They flew unannounced to the town where the two women lived and phoned Dorothy at the church to ask if she would have lunch with them alone.

Her mother tried to lay the blame on Edith. "Honey," she said, "can't you reason with Edith and help us to mend this relationship? You get along fine with her parents. We don't know what she's got against us."

Somehow, this irritated Dorothy, who responded: "Look, we may be part of the problem, but you are the other part. I'm caught in the middle. Just like today. You came here surreptitiously, without calling ahead, and asked me to meet you without Edith. Can't you imagine how that makes me feel? How it will make her feel when I tell her? Why don't you just go home and think about what you can do to make things better instead of demanding that I do something?"

Her parents were hurt and astounded. They didn't know how to deal with their daughter's new attitude, or which way to turn now that she had thrown the blame back on them. So they decided that the best thing was to lapse into silence and quit trying to maintain close contact with their daughter. They even went to a professional counselor for help.

"Don't blame yourselves," the counselor told them. "I've seen parents do this over and over. They reproach themselves for an estrangement instigated by their child. They think surely they could have prevented it or at least turned it around after it occurred. But you couldn't have even if you had made the effort. You can't win. You have to get used to that. You're getting enough abuse from your daughter and her partner, so don't add any more on yourselves. Try to get beyond this if you can. They want it this way and may never change."

Both sets of parents were amazed that Dorothy's church allowed them to stay on as pastor and partner. But the church obviously loved Dorothy, and the church had grown a lot under her ministry. So most of the people accepted Edith as well, especially after she started a preschool for working parents and took on a number of other jobs in the church.

Soon, other lesbian couples in the community began attending services, and the members appeared to accept them with genuine warmth. The church earned a reputation throughout the community as an openly friendly church for homosexuals, and, even though a few people were uncomfortable with this and left, they were soon replaced by socially active people who appreciated having an accepting institution in their town.

BABY MAKES THREE

After a couple of years, Edith began campaigning for Dorothy to agree for her to be artificially inseminated and start a family of their own. Then, following months of discussion and a few unsolicited comments from their siblings, Edith's parents, and the church board, they went against most of the advice and Edith became pregnant.

When the baby, a little girl, was born, Dorothy contacted her parents with the news that they were grandparents. It was the first time they had heard from her in more than a year, and her mother would have been much happier with the simple news that Dorothy wanted to mend the breach between them. But Dorothy didn't offer an apology for the estrangement. She only said she was calling to let them know about the baby, who was named for an aunt in Edith's family.

Their counselor warned them not to expect anything else, but Dorothy's parents both hoped and prayed for another call or even a surprise visit. They wanted badly to be part of their daughter's life and to meet their new granddaughter.

But nothing else happened.

And, two years later, Edith had twin boys.

Again Dorothy called her parents. She told them about the twins, but also indicated that Edith was gravely ill with an infection. Her mother was truly sorry, and expressed her feeling to Dorothy. They talked on the phone with Edith's parents, and learned that they had been out to visit her and had seen the boys.

"I'm going back again next week," said Edith's mother. "Why don't you go with me?"

As much as she wanted to say yes, Dorothy's mother declined. But she asked Edith's mother to keep her apprised of Edith's health.

Every day for twelve successive days, Dorothy's parents sent flowers and cards to Edith. There was no response. Then, one afternoon, the phone rang at the library, and it was Dorothy. She thanked her mother for her thoughtfulness and said, "Edith's mom's returning home tomorrow. Any chance you and Dad could take some time off and come to see us? I need help."

"Is Edith still in the hospital?" her mother asked.

"No. We brought her home yesterday."

"Sure, dear," she heard herself say. "I'll talk to your dad and we'll come as soon as we can."

When they arrived at Dorothy and Edith's home, two-year-old Marta won their hearts in the first five minutes. Dorothy let her lead them upstairs to see her new baby brothers. "This is Daniel and this is David," she said, gesturing exaggeratedly at each in turn. "I didn't know we were going to have two babies. There is only one of me!"

With the introductions behind them, Marta proceeded to lead them to the guest room where they would be staying. Dorothy had remained in the background, but now they turned to explain to her that they had made reservations at a nearby motel.

Marta didn't want them to leave. She locked her arms around her grandfather's leg and said, "You have to stay with Marta!"

Dorothy obviously wanted them to stay too, so they acquiesced and carried up their luggage.

Edith, who had been sleeping when they arrived, awoke and came into the living room to greet them. She seemed a little weak but was otherwise all right. They detected a certain frostiness in her voice as she thanked them for the flowers and cards, and realized right away that Edith would have preferred that they weren't there.

Nevertheless, they pitched in to help with the house, the cooking, and the baby chores.

It was only a couple of hours, though, before Edith began issuing instructions on how to do everything. Marta was to have only bottled water. All groceries were to be purchased at the Total Health Food Store. There were to be no fried foods. Martha couldn't go anywhere with them in the car. They could take her for a walk in the stroller, but only if she was properly strapped in and they didn't venture more than a few blocks from home.

Edith presented them with a long list of telephone numbers of doctors, hospitals, the poison control center, the police, the fire department, close friends, her own parents and siblings, and the church office. She lectured them about child safety as if it were a totally new subject to them.

When the time came for them to fly home, nobody was happier than they were. Their heads were reeling and their nerves were shot. They agreed that they had never been around such a demanding, controlling person in all their lives. And the worst part was, they also agreed, that they had never felt welcome, even though they had spent the whole time working like galley slaves!

TIME PRESENT

Marta and the twins are now in middle school. All three appear to be gifted, well-rounded students. Marta is extremely musical. She stays at the piano practicing until Edith actually shoos her away. "Most mothers have to beg their children to practice," she brags. "I beg mine to stop."

Daniel and David are interested in sports, especially tennis and soccer. Dorothy attends all their matches, and has employed a coach to work with them on their tennis game. She dreams that one of them will become a professional tennis player.

There is still a half-open door between Dorothy and Edith and Dorothy's parents. It is a strained relationship, but Dorothy's mother says that is better than nothing. When I asked her how she would characterize the relationship, she thought a minute, then said: "I feel as if Edith has built a high, thick wall around Dorothy and the children, and she alone controls the only gate between their home and ours. Is that silly? George and I have simply had to learn to be content with whatever occasional crumbs they toss our way."

"I've learned," she said a little later, "that one member of a lesbian couple can be as jealous of her mate's parents as the daughter-in-law in a heterosexual relationship. I don't know what happened to that adorable little blond child who practically lived at our house when Dorothy was growing up. When did we become the enemy?"

She shook her head and laughed a little ironic laugh. "No one ever prepared me for a life like this."

BEN AND LARRY

On the other hand, there are Ben and Larry. We've known them for thirty years. They were members of one of my husband's churches, and we have remained good friends with them even though we live across the country from them now.

They live in a fine neighborhood in an elegant three-story home that says "Welcome" the minute you step inside. They share their place unselfishly with church members who want to use it for formal dinners, committee meetings, or anything else. I know some of the people who pass through their doors don't really approve of same-sex partnerships. But Ben and Larry are so totally generous and outgoing that these people almost have to accept them, and most are glad to be numbered among their friends.

They also own a log house in the mountains that I personally think almost surpasses the one in the city. Windows across the back of the house open onto a spectacular view of the Sangre de Christo Mountains. It's a truly idyllic place. Ben and Larry both love it, because their work often becomes so heavy that they need a real change of scenery, which it affords. Ben is a clinical psychologist and Larry is a social worker. They take their work very seriously and are more than compassionate toward their clients. Having that mountain home has often preserved their sanity.

They met at university while Larry was working on a master's degree and Ben was pursuing his Ph.D. Each was drawn to the other by mutual affinities and a desire to help poor and suffering people. They discussed their ideas and class work, and what they wanted to do when they finished their degrees. Friends noticed how animated they became when they were together. Each seemed to evoke a special liveliness in the other.

Ben's parents were especially proud of him, as he was the first member of their family to go to college. His getting a doctorate was the icing on a three-layer cake. They were poor farmers and helped him all they could, but he basically paid for his own education by working after classes and winning scholarships.

He didn't forget his upbringing. On the farm, he had risen at four every morning to help with the feeding and milking. In the afternoons, he always did more chores before settling down to his homework. When he got to college, he just kept working, and he said it made him really appreciate his parents, who had instilled in him the virtues of work, learning, and love.

Larry's upbringing was different. He came from a wealthy family who had a maid, a cook, a nanny, and a gardener. The gardener also doubled as a chauffeur. His grandparents were wealthy too, and, as they made huge contributions to political campaigns, his father received various diplomatic assignments overseas. So Larry had often lived abroad as a child, and spoke three or four languages.

Fortunately, all his advantages didn't leave him spoiled or arrogant; in fact, they seemed to produce the opposite effect. He always felt a strong need to help people. When his family lived in Paris, he experienced a great sympathy for the *clochards*, the ragged street people who slept under the bridges and lived on handouts. In London and New York, he couldn't bear the sight of people sleeping in cardboard boxes during the winter-time. Nor could he endure the stories of blacks being attacked by dogs and fire hoses during the Civil Rights movement.

His parents always said his heart was going to explode one day because it was so full of other people's problems. When he said he was going to get a degree in social work, no one in his family was surprised. In fact, his father said he would have been surprised if he had done anything else.

Despite the fact that Ben and Larry came from opposite ends of the social spectrum, they had a lot in common. They both loved people and wanted to help the unfortunate. They shared a strong interest in the arts. Both were articulate and witty. And they had an equal appreciation of good food.

Larry's friends suspected he was gay, but they were surprised when he and Ben moved in together, as they hadn't thought Ben was.

When they decided to become partners, the two men vis-ited their parents to announce their sexual preference and say they had chosen to live together. Larry's parents seemed rather nonchalant about the whole matter, but it was definitely hard for Ben's folks to accept that he would not be marrying someone who could give them grandchildren. They were country folks and went to the United Methodist church in a little village near their farm, where people were less accustomed to seeing gay men. But they were also simple people given to openness and directness of expression, and after a couple of lengthy discussions with Ben they finally accepted what they realized they could not change and said that Larry would be welcome in their home.

INITIAL SIGNS OF TURBULENCE

It was after Ben's parents' third visit to their home that Larry began to display some signs of inner turmoil. He seemed somehow to be on the verge of anger, even though nothing had happened or been said that might have provoked his irritability.

Ben noticed the change in him and asked, "Are you coming down with some kind of bug?"

"No," said Larry. "I'm just feeling sort of antsy. I've got a lot on my mind that I need to discuss with you."

"Okay," said Ben, settling onto the sofa. "I'm all ears."

Larry had gotten only partway into his monologue of complaints about Ben's parents when Ben realized he wasn't ready to hear them, especially the ones pertaining to his mother. He had always been close to his mother, and didn't even like to think negative things about her.

"Wait a minute, Larry," he said, holding up his hands. "You seem to have a lot of grievances eating on you. Why don't you write down a list of them and let me have the list. Then we'll have a beer and discuss them."

So Larry made the list and they sat down to talk about what was on it.

"Number one," he began, "I need to be a happy person, but I'm not when I'm around your parents—especially your mother. Number two, your parents ignore me. I'm here to stay, they aren't. Number three, your parents have a damaging effect on our relationship. Number four, I'm tired of your mother's guilt over our lifestyle. She's been to a shrink, a couple of ministers, and God knows who else to help her understand us. We could have given her the information and support she needed, but obviously we aren't good enough for her. Number five, your mom has a lot of control over you. When she visits, I always lose confidence in myself. I'm afraid I'm going to lose you."

Ben told him he had gotten everything out of perspective. "You're overreacting to some totally insignificant statements my mother made. She means you no harm. In fact, she accepts you as a son. Think about it. Every time they visit, Mom makes some special recipe for you. She knows how much you love cooking for everyone, and she wants to make something just to please you. The first thing she says when we visit them is, 'Larry, come to the kitchen and taste the casserole. It's a new recipe, so give me your honest opinion.' You need to accept my mom and dad for who they are, and you'll enjoy them a lot more."

"While I'm on a roll here," he continued, "let me say that you have unrealistic expectations of them and yourself. Let up a little. Cut them some slack. They're never going to come between us. There's room in my heart for all of you, and you shouldn't ever feel crowded out in the least."

In the end, this kind of frankness eventually won out in Ben and Larry's relationship. But it didn't happen overnight. Larry continued to have misgivings for a long time, and he and Ben had a lot of discussions about it. Gradually, though, he realized that his commitment to Ben meant a commitment to his folks as well. And he loved Ben enough to want Ben to continue enjoying his parents as much as he liked, the way Ben allowed him to enjoy his.

When Ben's father died, Ben brought his mother to live

with them for a while. There were times when I thought this was going to undo all the growing Larry had done, as he often told me privately that he was exasperated with Ben's mom and wished she would fall down a deep well. But he managed to control his temper with her, and on the whole they developed a fairly good relationship.

I sometimes visited Ben's mother when the men were away from the house, and we had long talks about her feelings. She said she really liked Larry and was glad he and Ben had one another in their lives. It had taken her a few years, she said, to get used to the fact that Ben was gay and lived with a man, and she never talked about it to her friends back home. But she knew everybody needed somebody else to love and feel close to, and, if Ben couldn't have loved a woman, she was happy it was Larry and not somebody else.

I asked if she missed having grandchildren.

"Oh no," she said. "I have a lot of grandchildren by my other kids. So I haven't really missed anything."

Later, after she had moved back home, I asked Larry one day if he ever missed her. He smiled and said, "You know, it's funny, but sometimes I really do. Not often, mind you. But I'm glad I do, because I know it makes Ben feel good when I tell him I've been thinking about his mom or that I called up to wish her a happy birthday or something."

A SIMPLE MATTER OF COURAGE

The stories of these two same-gender couples suggest that the participants are all basically good people who want solid, reliable partnerships and are willing to work at them. But, as in the case of heterosexual couples, one person in each relationship became jealous of his or her partner's family—especially the mother—and attempted to impede the flow of affection between the partner and the partner's family. Each jealous partner typically wanted their mate's attention focused solely on them.

In Ben and Larry's case, because Ben stood up to Larry in behalf of his parents, the four of them were able to work out an acceptable relationship and Larry even grudgingly admitted a certain fondness for Ben's mother. In Dorothy and Edith's case, unfortunately, Dorothy did not stand up for her parents with Edith, but sided with Edith when she wanted to cut Dorothy's family out of their lives. As a result, the estrangement between Dorothy and her parents has never been fully resolved.

When two people marry or join as partners, they bring their families as well as themselves into the relationship. If one partner is weak and refuses to be his or her family's spokesperson, that family is left without representation at the table. When any kind of tension or misunderstanding arises, as it always will, that partner's parents are at an impossible disadvantage, for they have no way of presenting their side of things or negotiating for a better relationship.

This is the way it has been in our experience with our son and his wife. We feel that she regarded us from the very beginning as the enemy, and began even before they married to enlist our son's loyalty and affections against us. We were powerless to change the situation because the one person who could successfully have acted as a mediator or intercessor, our son, had taken the side of our accuser.

I think that's one reason I have always had such a strong admiration for Ben. I liked the way he stood up to Larry and said he intended to befriend both Larry *and* his parents. By showing courage at a crucial moment, he managed to preserve a good working relationship for all four of them.

Dorothy, on the other hand, turned out to be like the lion in *The Wizard of Oz*—he lacked courage. Because she didn't stand up to her partner the way Ben did, she and Edith sacrificed two of the best friends they could ever have had—her parents.

Our son and his wife lost the same thing, and for the very same reason. Our son didn't have the courage to stand up to Monica and argue for the inclusion of his parents in their future lives.

6

THE (UN)TAMING OF THE SHREW

> Of course my mother won. If my father had not given in he would have had to live with outraged female virtue for—perhaps the rest of his life.
>
> — Robertson Davies, *Fifth Business*

> All human beings are programmed for far more pathology than could possibly become manifest in a lifetime.
>
> — Edwin H. Friedman, *Generation to Generation*

> If I be waspish, best beware my sting.
>
> — Katharina, in Shakespeare's *The Taming of the Shrew*

IT HAPPENED YEARS AGO NOW. My husband was a university professor then and was out of town on a speaking trip. The phone rang in the middle of the night and I struggled to answer it. A sense of panic ran through me like an electric current. We never got phone calls at 1:30 A.M. Something must have happened to my husband!

"Hello."

"I want to speak to Dr. Killinger," said an anguished male

voice. "I'm going to commit suicide."

"Who is this?"

"It's Martin Thompson. Please! I need to talk to Dr. Killinger."

Martin Thompson...Martin Thompson...Martin Thompson...I knew I knew the name. Yes, he had been in our home for dinner. He was one of John's graduate students. A bright one, as I remembered.

"Please help me," he pled.

The house was freezing. Our boys were asleep. I knew nothing about counseling a suicidal person. What should I do? What would happen when he found out he couldn't speak to my husband?

Questions, I thought. I'll ask him questions so he'll have to keep talking. I got up and went to our bathroom, which had a heat grid under the tiles, and switched on the heat. Sitting on the floor, I began asking questions, one after another.

An hour went by. Maybe longer. He was talking incessantly now, but he was often incoherent. This made me nervous, even though I had finally managed to stop shivering.

Another hour passed, and another.

About 4 A.M., Martin's wife Ramona apparently entered the room and heard him talking. She screamed at him to hang up the phone. It was a loud, unearthly scream. She cursed and regaled him with every kind of accusation she could think of. Who was he talking to, she wanted to know. Was it a woman? Was it his doctor? It wouldn't do him any good.

She used words I had never heard before. Many of them sounded awful and vulgar.

Martin began to sob and tell me how worthless he was. He whimpered like a whipped puppy. My heart was aching for him.

Ramona kept screaming at him and trying to tear the phone

away from him. Then she threw things. I could hear glass breaking and thumping noises against the walls. Eventually her tirade wore her down, but not before she released one final salvo against the poor man.

"I'm filing for a divorce, you f———ing son of a bitch!" she screamed. "If you want to commit suicide, I'll help you. I hate you, goddamn you! Your son hates you. So do your parents. I've seen to that. Tell whoever that is on the phone how you've wrecked our lives. You are nothing but a filthy, lowdown, f———g scumbag!"

I heard a door slam, and she was gone.

Martin and I continued talking till sunrise. He had become calm enough for me to ask if it was all right for me to hang up and call another of my husband's former students for help, a minister named Jim who was pastor of a church across town. I knew he and Martin had been friends in graduate school, and Martin had served as an intern in Jim's church.

Martin thanked me. He said he would like to talk with Jim.

The minute we hung up, I phoned Jim.

Martin now lived more than four hundred miles away, in another state. But Jim didn't hesitate. He canceled his appointments for the day and drove to Martin's home. After having a cup of coffee with him, he took him to an institution where Martin was hospitalized.

When he returned home after six weeks, Ramona rode him harder than ever. Now he bore the added stigma, in her eyes, of having had electroconvulsive shock therapy. She called him "crazy," "loony," and said he had gone "around the bend." Before long, he became ill again, and went back to the hospital.

A pattern emerged. Martin would have more ECT treatments and Ramona would be more abusive than before. Then he would return for more treatments and come home to more abuse.

Eventually Ramona sued for divorce and moved back home with her parents. Martin remained under professional care for several years, but eventually regained a sense of personal worth and dignity. He applied for and got a position as a counselor in a Midwestern hospital.

I have always wondered about Martin. Why he married Ramona in the first place—why he put up with her abusive treatment for so long—why he didn't fight back and defend himself against her endless tirades. Ramona was clearly a shrew, a woman who thrived on mistreating her husband. But what is it that binds husbands, who are usually physically larger and stronger than their wives, to women like Ramona? Why don't they simply walk away from them?

Marriage is a mutual affair in which two people learn to accommodate one another's peculiarities for the sake of the joys and happiness they find together. If one of the persons, male or female, is consistently abusive, why do they remain together? We know that women often cling to the men who mistreat them for the simple reason that they are financially dependent on them and have nowhere to turn. But why should a man remain with a woman who wants to destroy him?

My husband and I have never understood why our son Richard has allowed himself to be so totally dominated by Monica. It is easy enough to say, "Well, she's very rich, and he doesn't want to give up the money." But before he met her he enjoyed living frugally. It was a kind of daily triumph to him. He actually prided himself on not needing more.

The mind-control answer is as good as we've come up with. It's more than the money in his case. Somehow Monica has managed to convince him, in that part of the brain where he has his self-identity, that who he is and how happy he is depends completely on her and her approval. She's a tall, strong woman, but no taller and certainly no stronger than Richard, who has the rippling muscles of a beach Adonis. The place where she is stronger than he is in her will. As an adult, he always seemed laid back and easy-going. But she isn't. She's as fierce and un-yielding as an oak post.

I'm glad Martin finally got away from his termagant wife. He and my husband still correspond by e-mail, and he has grown into a happy, thoughtful man. In addition to his work at the hospital, he now has a small church that he pastors, and the work gives him great satisfaction. After a few years of being on his own, he remarried. His second wife, Alma, is a former psychiatric nurse, and she understands what he went through with Ramona and tries to compensate for it by being invariably sweet and gentle.

A daughter by his first wife is now grown and has a child of her own, a little boy who is the apple of Martin's eye. Alma encourages the daughter and grandchild to come for visits, and when they do she treats them so generously that they actually prefer coming to their home instead of Ramona's.

Not every ill-treated male comes off so luckily.

BILL AND LENA

A few months ago we had lunch with our friends, Jan and Wayne, who live only a couple of towns away from ours. They were feeling dispirited about their son Bill and his wife Lena. They had flown out to Salem, Oregon, to spend Thanksgiving with them and the visit had turned into a fiasco. That wasn't a total surprise. Jan said she knew their relationship with their son and his wife since they married was only minimally okay, but she and Wayne went hoping for the best.

"We made a little pact before we left," she said, "that no matter what happened we were going to make things work."

Oh my, I thought to myself, how many times have we parents of sons voiced that very determination?

Over a meal of sweet-and-sour chicken and stir-fried vegetables, we listened to Jan and Wayne's story. They landed in Salem, they said, and rented a car.

Why, I wondered, after they flew all the way across country to see their children, didn't the children pick them up at the airport?

They found their son and daughter-in-law's condo, which was on the second story of a building without an elevator, and carried their luggage up to the door. Wayne pushed the doorbell button. Bill answered it promptly, as if he had been waiting on the other side of the door.

"Oh," he said, "you've brought your luggage up."

He stumbled around in search of the right words, and finally said he was sorry but he and Lena didn't really have enough room for them in the condo. They'd have to go to a nearby motel.

"Besides," Bill added, "Lena's pregnant and doesn't need the added stress of company right now."

"I was ready to turn around and go home right then," said Jan. "I knew from an earlier description of their condo that they had a guest bedroom. But we had promised we would try to keep the peace, and I remembered. So I said sweetly, 'Oh, poor thing! Of course she doesn't. We'll just go get settled somewhere and then we'll come back.' But my mind was leaping all over the place. Wayne and I were going to be grandparents. I couldn't believe it. I guess I'd have forgiven Lena anything at that point—even putting us out in the cold when they had that extra bedroom!"

"Uh, you may have some trouble finding a place," said Bill. "You know, the holiday and all. So we won't expect you back until about supper time."

"With that charitable send-off," said Wayne, "we lugged our bags back down to the rental car and started driving around. It wasn't hard to find a room, despite the fact it was almost the holidays. We found a nice Comfort Inn a few blocks away and got a king-size room at a reasonable rate."

"Then Wayne called Bill and told him," said Jan. Here her face became very impassioned.

"You know what Bill said?" she asked. "He said, 'Don't bother to come back here today. There's a nice Olive Garden down the street from the Comfort Inn. Lena's been craving Italian food since she got pregnant. We'll meet you there at seven o'clock.'"

"You're kidding," my husband said.

"I kid you not," she said. "We had flown all the way across the country to see them, and that—that—I'd better not say what she is—didn't want us in their condo, even for drinks before dinner."

"How was it at dinner?" I asked.

Jan took a deep breath. "Well, for starters, it was already ten p.m. our time back home, so we were both starved and not feeling like eating. But of course our son and daughter-in-law wouldn't have thought about anything so mundane as that. She—Lena—had had a nice long nap that afternoon, and she was all abuzz when they got to the restaurant. But it was all too artificial. I mean, she talked like butter wouldn't melt in her mouth, and said how sweet it was of us to fly all the way out to see them, and all that, but you could tell she was just faking it, trying to make Bill think she was the dutiful little daughter-in-law."

"Then the waiter came to take our orders," said Wayne.

"I was getting to that," said Jan. "He said he was there to take our drink orders, and Wayne looked at the wine list and ordered a nice bottle of wine. You know, it was supposed to be a kind of celebration for our new grandchild, and all that. Well, when he left—the waiter, I mean—Lena just exploded. I mean it was like she was a firecracker and somebody had lit her fuse and it had burned down and gone boom!

"Her remarks were aimed at Bill, but it was obvious that we were the reason for them. 'Bill,' she said in that kind of shrill little voice of hers, 'it was not very thoughtful of you all to order wine when you know I'm not supposed to drink any. You know my doctor doesn't want me to drink anything. I would appreciate it, when the waiter comes back, if you would send it back so that I don't have to smell it. I'm not sure I could eat a bite if I smelled everybody around me having wine and I couldn't have a drop."

I couldn't wait to hear what happened.

"Well, Bill spoke to the waiter as he came back with the wine and four glasses and told him his wife couldn't drink anything because she was pregnant, and would he please not give him a glass either. The waiter looked a little flustered and apologetic, but it was clear he didn't know what to do."

"So what did you do?" I asked. "Did you refuse yours too?"

"I sort of kept mum to see what Wayne was going to do, but he let the waiter set a glass in front of him and start to open the bottle, so I didn't say anything and let him give me a glass too. It was pretty tense for a while, but I'm glad he stuck to his guns. We don't drink very much, but we always enjoy a glass of Chianti or Merlot with an Italian meal."

Wayne spoke up in his defense. "I wasn't going to allow a

pouty, selfish, three-months-pregnant daughter-in-law to dictate to me about whether I could have a glass of wine with my meal. She could at least have said something when I first ordered the wine."

"So how did the rest of the visit go?" my husband asked.

Jan raised her eyebrows as if that were a sufficient answer.

"The evening didn't get any better," she finally proceeded. "There were so many things I wanted to know, but Little Miss Priss was in a mood to guard her secrets, and didn't tell us much about anything. They hadn't yet learned the sex of the baby, but she knew it was going to be a girl because she had prayed for a daughter. Had they picked out a name? Well, yes and no. They had thought about Emily Ann because her best friend in college was named Emily, and they were also considering Rachel Sue because her mother's name was Sue, but they hadn't really decided. Bill just sat there, looking stupid, while I asked questions that got answers like that. And about eight-thirty she yawned and said she needed to get home and get her beauty rest, because she said she always got real tired now that she was carrying a baby, as if nobody else in the world had ever done it."

Wayne was chasing the final bits of rice on his plate. When he had cornered and devoured them, he laid down his chopsticks, wiped his mouth, and put his napkin by the plate. There was a kind of finality about his actions.

"Okay, Wayne," my husband said. "Tell us the rest of the story."

"Rest of story," he said, musing. "Okay. For two days, we sat in that damned motel room and the only contact we had with our son was a couple of calls from his cell phone while he was driving to and from work. I suggested he come by our motel to visit with us, or have lunch with us, but he said he didn't think he ought to, that Lena might drive by and see his car."

My husband pulled a long face in sympathy.

"We almost flew back home," said Jan. "Wayne wanted to. But it would have cost us more than the motel was costing to do it, so I talked him into staying. We found a couple of nice malls, and spent some time shopping."

"And that was it?" I asked. "Your visit to Salem, Oregon?"

Wayne shook his head. "On Thanksgiving morning, we got a call from Bill. Apparently he had shamed Lena into at least having us over for the day. But when we got there—what was it, Jan, about ten o'clock?—there wasn't any food smell in the house. She hadn't fixed a damn thing. They were waiting for Jan to come in and make their Thanksgiving dinner!"

"No!" I exclaimed.

Jan bobbed her head affirmatively. "So help me, God. Every bit of it. She didn't even move her keister off the sofa to peel the carrots!"

"How did it go?" I asked.

"Well, it was a good dinner," said Wayne, "in spite of how we felt about the way we were being treated. And Billy and Lena got a little friendlier after they'd stuffed their guts. But I'd had enough. We weren't supposed to fly home till Sunday, but I called up and got our reservations changed to Friday. I wasn't going to stay where we weren't wanted a day longer than I had to. We'd seen our boy, we knew he was going to be a father and we were going to be grandparents, and that was it. Time to go home."

"Tell them about Friday," said Jan. "When we left."

Wayne smiled a wry little smile.

"Well," he said, "we drove by the condo. Our flight was that night, so we went by after Billy got home from work. He was surprised to see us and to learn we were leaving. He said he thought he'd see us the next day, which was Saturday. But ol'

Lena, she just sat there on the sofa painting her toenails and didn't even look up at us. We talked to Bill and looked over at her occasionally, but she never bothered to take her eyes off her feet."

"And when we told Bill we were on the way to the airport to go home," added Jan, "he said he thought that was a good idea, that we'd be glad to get home. Just like that. No 'Oh, please stay, I wanted us to do something tomorrow.' Just 'Okay, so you're going home.'"

"We gave Billy a goodbye hug," said Wayne, "and I guess we'd have given her one too, only she never took her eyes off her damned toenails. So we left and got home in the wee hours of the morning. I was worn out but glad to get back. It'll be a cold day on the Fourth of July if I ever go back out to see that couple, even after our grandchild is born."

"Were you mad at yourselves for having gone?" I asked.

They looked at one another. "Damn right," said Wayne. "We were chumps."

THE SECOND INNING

We had lunch with Jan and Wayne again a couple of weeks ago in the same Chinese restaurant. This time they told us about their second visit to Salem, Oregon—even though Wayne had sworn they'd never go back.

Bill and Lena's baby had come—a boy, whom they named Kevin—and they had been dying to meet their first grandchild. They had talked a couple of times with Bill, who, as always, called from his cell phone in his car, and knew that Lena's mother, Katherine, had been invited to stay with them for two months when the baby came so she could help Lena around the house. That meant there was no question of their staying there, but that didn't bother them as they hadn't expected to anyway after the last visit.

Bill told them that he and Lena really wanted them to come. Lena's mother had other grandchildren, so this was not as spectacular an occasion for her, but as little Kevin was their first grandchild she wanted it to be a special event for them.

"I guess we're getting soft in the head," said Jan. "We thought, 'Oh good, Lena's finally growing up now that she has a child, and maybe we'll develop a real relationship with her after all.' Foolish me."

Wayne was nodding quietly.

"So what happened?" asked my husband.

"I'll let Jan tell you," said Wayne.

"We flew to Salem, rented a car, and checked into the Comfort Inn like before," she said. "Wayne phoned Bill and asked what would be a good time for us to come over. He suggested about six, after he got in from work. So we waited until a little after six, then drove over and rang the doorbell.

"Bill came to the door and led the way back to the kitchen, where he was making supper. On our way, I happened to look through the partially open door into the living room and saw Lena sitting on the floor with an older woman near her. It was Katherine, Lena's mother. Lena had the baby in her arms and was breast feeding her.

"I don't know what came over me, but I thought I couldn't wait another minute to meet my grandson. So I pushed the door open and stepped in. But when Jan looked up and saw me, she said, 'Oh f--k!,' passed little Kevin over to her mother, and promptly got up and left the room."

"She didn't!" exclaimed Wayne.

"I didn't tell you," Jan said apologetically. "I was so ashamed of it that I kept it to myself."

"Did you tell Bill?" he asked.

"No. I didn't tell anybody. I was too embarrassed. It was like I had the plague or something."

I think I could have predicted before they told us that this visit wasn't much more rewarding than their previous one. The only bonus was that they did get to see their grandson four times in three days for about ten minutes at each viewing. Lena permitted Jan to hold him once, but took him back a minute or two later, saying it was time for his nap and she needed to put him to bed.

"At least we've seen him," said Wayne.

"Yes," said Jan, "and we probably won't see him again until he graduates from high school."

I understood how they both felt. I got to see my second grandchild about as much as they got to see Kevin, and haven't seen my third and fourth grandchildren at all.

ALAN AND VERONICA

But now let me tell you about Alan, a young man I've known since birth. Alan was an adorable, chubby, red-cheeked little shaver whose feet were always in perpetual motion. He had a quiet, low-keyed mother and a loud, high-strung father. But no matter what was happening around him, Alan wore a captivating smile that invariably melted everybody's heart. He was almost too good a child to be true.

Alan's home was always full of tension, mostly because of his dad, who was constantly ill at ease and overbearing at the same time. Alan wasn't allowed to make decisions unless his dad prescreened them and gave him only two choices from which to pick. By the time he was a teenager, the restrictions his dad imposed made him nervous too. His mother said once that he was "as jumpy as frog legs in a skillet." But he never lost his fetching smile and sweet nature. Any time we were around him and his family, I had the urge to strangle his father. I always thought that such a brutish, insensitive man had never done anything to deserve a lovely son like Alan.

When he graduated from the university, Alan came back and lived in a small house close to his parents' home. I thought he must be like the dog that licks the hand of the person who beats it, and was too attached to his folks to get far away from them. He went to work for a realty company, where his confidence seemed to grow by leaps and bounds with each property he sold. His own little house became his pride and joy, and he decorated it slowly and meticulously, often with ideas he got from other homes he visited.

One of Alan's fellow agents had a beautiful daughter named Veronica. She looked like a Hollywood starlet, and from everything I could gather her mind was already set on having the things a starlet might acquire. Alan was immediately smitten with her, but she didn't reciprocate his feelings until he began to become a very successful agent and it was apparent that he was going to do very, very well in business. Then she began to find him increasingly attractive. When she looked at him, she probably saw her dream house with a swimming pool, her double closet overflowing with expensive clothes, her jewelry box filled with rings and necklaces, and a sleek new Lexus in the driveway.

To make a long story short, she set her cap for Alan, and it wasn't long before he was hooked and reeled in.

After Veronica and Alan had the wedding she desired, complete with a white limo that looked as long as a bus, she set about the task of changing everything about him. She did it so quickly and smoothly that it was almost as if she had been planning her agenda even before they got engaged.

One thing that remained fixed on their agenda from before the wedding was dinner with his parents and sister every week. His parents were looking forward to adding a place at table for Veronica, because at that point she was still playing the loving, good-natured woman whose primary aim in life was to make her new husband happy.

"Aren't we lucky?" said Ruth, Alan's mother. "On a scale of one to ten, I give Veronica a ten and a half!"

Even his father Adam, who tended to be very critical, couldn't find fault with Veronica.

Before long, though, they began to sing a different song. They learned that whenever Veronica was around she tended to create little irritations that annoyed them like a case of hives. For example, she made fun of their furniture. "It's so common," she told Alan in front of them. "We want something much finer than this."

She ridiculed Ruth's clothes and let her know that her own mother's cooking was much superior to hers.

One day Ruth came downstairs to go to lunch with them wearing a red dress. Veronica looked horrified. "That red dress is so out of style," she said. "But if you must wear it, dear, at least wear a complimentary shade of lipstick."

Then, after a moment's hesitation, she added, "Actually, Ruth, you're too old to wear red."

Then things got ratcheted up a notch by Veronica's tendency to misrepresent what Ruth had said or done to her. Ruth knew it was happening, but felt powerless to stop her. Their relationship became poisoned by a host of little lies Veronica told Alan. And the worst part was that Alan appeared to believe them.

Eventually Veronica got what she wanted: they stopped visiting Alan's parents. Ruth was hurt and mystified. "I don't understand," she said. "We were all so happy before she came into the picture. Now everything seems dirty or something."

Adam, more forthright, said simply that Alan always did mess things up, and he guessed he had done it again by choosing somebody like Veronica.

Meanwhile, Veronica spent, spent, spent. In addition to the Lexus Alan used in his business, she had to have a BMW. Soon she was campaigning for a new and larger house. "You sell much nicer homes than this every day," she would say to Alan. "Why can't we have one of those too?"

So eventually Alan gave in and they moved to a much larger house. Then Veronica had to have it remodeled and wanted a swimming pool and new landscaping in the backyard.

Alan wanted children, but Veronica didn't. She was having too much fun, she said, to louse up her life with kids. Part of her fun involved seeing a couple of older men she'd met at the country club. Both were rich and successful. When Alan heard from friends that she was running around with them, he questioned her about it. She only laughed and told him he wasn't any fun.

As things worsened, Alan became depressed. When he was young, his father had often pushed him to the point where he lost his self-confidence. Now his wife was humiliating him by her behavior and the insolence with which she responded to his knowledge of what she was doing. He confessed to Ruth one day when he dropped by for coffee that he thought he was at the end of his rope.

It wasn't long after that when he came home one day and discovered that his garage opener didn't work. He got out and tried his key in the front door of the house, but it didn't work either. He couldn't figure out what was wrong. He rang the bell and pounded on the door, because he had seen Veronica's car in the garage and knew she was there. But no one came to the door. He got back in his car and used his cell phone to call Veronica.

"What's going on?" he asked.

"Oh dear, I guess I forgot to tell you," she said in a chirrupy voice. "My lawyer advised me to have the locks changed. And there's a court order for you to stay away from this house, lovey. So I guess you'd better leave before I call 911."

She laughed and hung up.

Later, it came to light that Veronica had inflicted a superficial wound on her shoulder with a kitchen knife and had gone to the police and accused Alan of having done it, so that there would be a police record of his "brutality."

Alan's bad dream had turned into a nightmare. He spent the next two months in legal hassles. His business associates were almost as upset as he was, because they got daily bulletins on Veronica's latest efforts to ruin her husband. Even Veronica's mother was upset by what she was doing. She admitted she knew her daughter was ambitious and greedy, but she said she had never known her to be so flagrantly mean and avaricious.

In the end, Alan lost a great deal of what he had saved and worked for. He might have done better, he admitted, but he didn't have the stomach to continue the fight. He signed off on a bad settlement merely to get Veronica out of his life. He bought a small condo from a client he was representing and started over, trying to put his life together again. Eventually he began dating a girl at the office named Lynn, and a couple of years later they married.

I saw him recently in a mall. There he was, coming toward me wearing that signature smile of his and holding a small boy's hand as he walked. A pretty woman held the boy's other hand.

"This is Damon," he said. "Damon, tell Mrs. Killinger how old you are."

Damon held up three fingers, checked them to be sure he had the right number exposed, then thrust them high in the air. "I'm *free!*" he exclaimed.

Then Alan introduced Lynn and we chatted a few minutes. I didn't mention the past, or what a long way he had come since that fateful wedding to Veronica. But it was obvious that he was at last happy with a new wife and a beautiful little boy.

I asked about his mother, and Alan said she was fine. "And your dad?" I asked.

He gave a little twist to his head, raised an eyebrow, and said, "Well, you know dad. You've known him a long time."

"Yes," I admitted, I had.

I thought about Alan for days after seeing him in his happier circumstances, and remembered what he had gone through with Veronica. Why is it, I wondered, that so many nice young men fall victim to women like her? It never seems to happen to callous, brutish young men. Always to the sensitive ones, the kind and gentle ones, like our son Richard. Do these evil, bitchy women have some kind of built-in radar to detect which men they can dominate and twist to their own selfish purposes?

My thoughts naturally went to a couple named Peter and Leslie, who were just starting down the same road that Alan and Veronica had traveled.

PETER AND LESLIE

My husband and I are friends of Peter's parents, whom I'll call James and Elizabeth. We all like the food at a particular

Mexican restaurant, and go there about once a month to catch up with what's going on in one another's lives. We tell them about Richard and Monica, and they tell us about Peter and Leslie.

Peter is in training to be a minister. He was in seminary in North Carolina, and held down a full-time job while getting his education. He met Leslie at the seminary while she was working on a master's degree in Christian education. They fell in love and decided not to wait to get married. Maybe when they both got their degrees, they thought, they could get called to the same church. Peter could be the congregation's minister and Leslie would be their minister of Christian education.

When they got their degrees, there was only one church willing to take on both of them in salaried positions. It was in Birmingham, Alabama, and was a nice suburban church with a fair-sized congregation. They were delighted to be able to serve the same church, and happily packed up their belongings and moved to Birmingham.

The next spring, Leslie gave birth to a baby girl. James and Elizabeth said she was ecstatic about being a mother. When they visited to meet their granddaughter, whose name was Deirdre, she was on top of the world. God had given her a wonderful husband, a great job, and a little miracle for her to love, she said.

A couple of years later, Peter and Leslie had a son, Robert, to keep little Deirdre company. And again Leslie professed that life was so much more wonderful than she had ever imagined it could be.

Everything was going beautifully for them. The church people seemed to love them, and they felt the same way about the church people. They had a nice home. They liked Birmingham. And they adored their two children.

But a year or so later, Peter began to see a change in Leslie.

For some reason, she began to be very critical of everything. She began by complaining about what the church expected of her as minister of education. Then it was what Peter expected of her as a wife and mother. He mentioned this to his parents because he thought she was going through a phase of new motherhood and thought his parents could corroborate his suspicion.

Elizabeth said she expected that was all it was. But she and James didn't really know what to think.

Leslie grew more and more critical, and began to complain about what she saw as Peter's great shortcomings. If anything went wrong at church, she blamed him for being a poor administrator. If she missed an appointment or was late to a meeting, she said her husband had let her down by not being home to keep the children as he had promised. One day when she was under pressure to get a retreat organized, she shouted at Peter that his church didn't own her and neither did he!

As Peter discussed this change in her with his parents, he confessed also that Leslie was beginning to tell lies to people in the church. They were usually small lies to cover her failure to get some assignment done, but it nevertheless concerned him, as she had never done this before.

James and Elizabeth, who were retired from the ministry themselves, understood about pressures from the congregation and suggested that maybe Leslie was tired of trying to manage a home and her job as well. They asked if Peter took her out on dates any more, or did anything to make her feel special the way he had before they married.

Prodded by his parents, he resolved to make an attempt to "court" his wife again. He started planning some outings, once a week, when they would dress up, go out to dinner without the children, and then go to a play, a concert, or a movie.

They were into this dating program a month when James

and Elizabeth went to visit them for a few days. Peter was excited, as they hadn't actually stayed with them more than overnight since the children had come. And James and Elizabeth were almost ecstatic about spending some time with their two grandchildren.

But Leslie didn't seem exactly overjoyed about their being there. It seemed to annoy her that they were having such a good time with Deirdre and Robert. "My goodness, don't carry on so," she said to them once when they were laughing with the children. "We've sent you loads of pictures and videos. Isn't that enough?"

James and Elizabeth hoped she wasn't feeling as quarrelsome with them as her tone made it sound. But by the second day of their visit, the tone was getting worse. Nothing they did with the children or to help with the load around the house seemed to satisfy her. And when James suggested at dinner one night that Peter and Leslie take a week's vacation somewhere together and let them stay with the children, she went ballistic.

"Don't you think I can take care of my home and work at the same time?" she demanded. "Well, I can! I've always taken care of my responsibilities, ever since I was young. Maybe you don't think I'm a fit wife to your son, but I wish you'd take a look at him sometime and see if you think he's the paragon of all virtues you've always accepted him as being!"

The parents tried to placate her and help her to see that they weren't being critical at all, they just liked their grandchildren and would be happy to have a chance to care for them while the couple got away. But there appeared to be no mending of the breach they had inadvertently caused, so they decided after another day to pack their bags and head for home.

Peter later apologized to them and admitted that he had lived hard after their visit.

"I don't understand what's happening," he said. "She's that way most of the time now. She seems to think you and I are in league against her, and think she isn't a good mother to the children. I don't know this Leslie. She's not the girl I married, I know that. Something has happened to her."

On his father's advice, Peter tried to get Leslie to go to a counselor. But she became upset whenever he brought up the possibility.

"Look, hon," he said to her, "we send people from our church to counselors all the time. People just need them from time to time. I think you may need one now. I'll go with you if you want me to. But I believe you need to see somebody. You're not behaving like yourself these days."

Again Leslie went ballistic, the way she had when her in-laws were visiting. Peter said he couldn't understand it. She had become so unreasonable that he could no longer talk to her about anything serious. She seemed to fly off the handle at the least provocation.

We listened to James and Elizabeth talk about their concern for their son and his wife and thought about our own son and daughter-in-law. At least Peter hadn't succumbed so totally to Leslie's behavior that he had become alienated from his parents. We told them they could be thankful for that.

A few months later, we learned of another installment in Peter and Leslie's lives. He had found out, said his parents, that Leslie was having an affair with the minister of a church in a nearby county. Leslie had met him at a youth retreat and they had fallen in love. Peter had suspected something like this when he happened to see the two of them in a restaurant one day and Leslie had become very befuddled when he went over and sat down at their table. Finally, a few days later, she had admitted to Peter that she was in love with someone else and he asked if it was her minister friend. She said yes, that her friend was going to get a divorce and she wanted one too.

Suddenly things that had made no sense began to seem more reasonable. If Leslie was unhappy with him, maybe that explained her increasing short-temperedness with him, a volatility that had led him to withdraw more and more from engaging her. He went to a counselor friend and talked about his situation. The counselor tried to help him prepare for what the counselor thought was inevitable, that they would end up in divorce court and Peter would probably have to leave his pastorate. Still, Peter hoped and prayed, it wouldn't come to that. Perhaps he could reason with Leslie and the other minister about their callings and what that meant in terms of their love and behavior toward one another.

But one night when Peter came in from work he received the shock of his life. It had been a long day that included a committee meeting over dinner, and he was looking forward to getting home, having a hot bath, and relaxing with the children until their bedtime. He noticed when he went up on the front porch that there were no lights on. Curious, he thought. Maybe Leslie had taken the children to the mall or something. Maybe they had gone out for supper.

He called out, but there was no answer. He went into the kitchen and turned on the light. There was a note from Leslie taped to the refrigerator.

She and her minister friend, the note said, were taking the children to Canada. By the time he found the note, they would be halfway there, and he couldn't stop them. They were going to start a new life, she said, and he shouldn't ever expect to see her or the children again.

Peter said he was so frantic and nauseated as he read the note that he fell across the kitchen table and screamed. He

couldn't believe it. His children were gone. His first thought
was that he would contact a lawyer in his church and get them
back. But how? He telephoned his parents and asked if they
could come and be with him. They wanted to know what had
happened. Reluctantly, he told them and read the note to them.
James said to hold on, they'd be there the next day.

He and Elizabeth had known something was wrong, they
said. They thought Leslie was having mental problems. But they
hadn't guessed it might be another man. Not Leslie. Not a minister of education in a church. Not their grandchildren's mother.

James and Elizabeth went with Peter to visit the attorney.
There was some talk of extradition and other methods of procedure. But the attorney warned Peter that it wouldn't be easy.
Leslie was the children's mother, and courts usually went along
with them. He even suggested that Leslie might concoct some
cock-and-bull story about Peter's having molested the children
if they attempted to get them back. The immediate decision
was to do nothing for a while, but to wait and see what Leslie
said or did.

The months dragged on. Peter got an uncontested divorce
from Leslie. His church seemed very understanding at first, but
gradually people began to suggest that it didn't feel right having
a minister whose wife had deserted him, and perhaps he should
consider finding another position. Eventually he found a job in
the offices of his denomination, where marital standing didn't
mean as much. The next time he heard from Leslie, she had left
the minister she had run off with and needed money. That was
the only reason she had contacted him. She wanted him to agree
to pay child support so she could move back to the States with
them. He said he would do it, but used his leverage as a means
of getting to see the children again.

"I don't guess we'll ever see them ourselves," bemoaned Elizabeth.

I could be thoroughly sympathetic with her, inasmuch as I don't get to see my grandchildren either. When you doubt if you'll ever know your own flesh and blood that way, you feel as if someone has cut your heart open and stuck an ice cube in it.

CHUCK AND VICKI

One more story in a similar vein. It comes from our years of living in Nashville, where my husband taught at Vanderbilt University.

My very best friend during those years was a woman named Connie. Connie was witty, intelligent, upbeat, and caring. We had a standing lunch date every week to discuss our concerns about our children, the community, and our respective churches—and also the latest news about her sister Vicki.

If I hadn't known Connie as well as I did, I would have thought her stories about Vicki were made up. Some of them were so awful that I would catch myself watching Connie's mouth move and hearing her voice when my mind wasn't computing what she said. My mental reject button kept deleting her narrative until I made my usual comment, "Look, Connie, tell me that again, and go slowly this time."

Connie and Vicki had been raised by a single mom. Their father died when Vicki was sixteen and Connie was six. Life hadn't been easy for any of them. Connie had always been content with what they had, but Vicki had apparently always wanted more. Being the elder, Vicki thought she was entitled to boss Connie when their mother was at work. She liked to remind Connie that her parents hadn't wanted her, and she often told lies on Connie to her mother and was gleeful if they got her into trouble.

Sometimes their mother would leave two Baby Ruth candy bars on the kitchen table as treats for the girls after school. Vicki often grabbed both bars and devoured them, smacking her lips exaggeratedly and taunting Connie by saying, "Don't you wish you had some of this yummy candy?" Then, as a reminder of what she would do if Connie reported this to their mother, she would dig her sharp fingernails into Connie's arm until they drew blood. Connie grew up feeling helpless to fend off her attacks or deal with her untruths.

If Vicki was an abominable little girl, she became a real monster when she reached adulthood. Marriage and parenthood seemed to make her even worse than before. As she grew older, she became more and more ill-tempered and violent.

Connie loved her brother-in-law Chuck, a rugged, six-foot-two, handsome fellow who she said was so generous he would give you the shirt off his back. Once, in the wintertime, he had actually taken off a new jacket he had received for Christmas and given it to a street person who didn't have a coat. "His heart was as big as all outdoors!" said Connie admiringly.

"I was glad when they got married," Connie admitted, "because it meant a lot more peace in our apartment. But I remember feeling sorry for Chuck at the time because I knew she would be mean to him. She was really the Queen of Mean, or whatever it is they call Leona Helmsley. Chuck was so good to Mom and me. He treated us as if we were special people. But he always paid a price when he did something nice for us. Vicki couldn't stand it that he and I got along so well."

Chuck and Vicki had moved into a house that belonged to his father. It was a few doors down the street from where his father and mother lived. Chuck liked having them so close, because he was finishing his university degree—a master's in broadcast journalism—and also working at the same time, and he thought Vicki would be safe staying alone at night that close to his folks.

Chuck had been in the national guard, and when the war in Korea began he was called up and sent to boot camp in California. Vicki remained in their house, but didn't get along with Chuck's parents, so she got lonely there. She asked their mother to send Connie down to spend the summer with her.

"It was murder," Connie told me. "Two months of her outlandish behavior. But I enjoyed getting to know Chuck's parents. They were nice. Sometimes they would take me out at night and buy me an ice cream cone. They asked Vicki too, of course, but she would never go with them. She said she hated them."

When Chuck was dispatched to Korea, he had two weeks' leave to visit Vicki and his parents. His parents, Connie said, were broken up about his leaving for the battlefield. They worried that something would happen and they would never see him again.

"But Vicki—Vicki was something else." Connie shook her head as she told it. "All she did was complain to Chuck about his leaving her there near his parents, and how awful they were to her. Her parting words to him at the train station were 'You'll pay for this.' I know it sounds cruel, but I heard her myself. That's what she said."

"And you know what Chuck's parents said?" she continued. "I overheard them talking. They said it was bad enough their son was going to war, but what they hated most was the miserable, hangdog look he had on his face from the mistreatment he received from Vicki!"

Chuck was slightly wounded in Korea and got frostbite on his toes, but otherwise he made it through the war okay and came home to finish his degree in journalism, this time courtesy of Uncle Sam and the GI Bill. He got a big job with an eastern network center and traveled all over the world covering stories. When he had been working for the network about a year, he bought Vicki a lovely home in a suburb near his base.

Now, because Chuck was gone so much on assignments, Vicki still insisted that their mother send Connie to stay with her for the summers and help look after her children, two sons and a daughter.

Connie loved being around Chuck, and when he was home he was as good to her as ever. But Vicki was even more diabolical than before, and treated Connie as a virtual slave around the house, forcing her to do the cleaning, the shopping, and much of the cooking, in addition to looking after the children and generally performing all the duties Vicki herself should have done.

One time, Connie remembered, Vicki had gone to bed with what she said was a migraine headache and spent the afternoon watching TV. Connie was in the kitchen preparing dinner. She opened the refrigerator door, and for some reason, when she did, the handle fell off onto the floor. There wasn't much she could do to fix it, as she had the baby girl on one hip and one of the boys was holding onto her leg as she moved around the kitchen.

Feeling desperate for one so young, Connie called out to Vicki to come and help her.

"Vicki came in angry," she recollected. "And when she saw the refrigerator handle lying in the middle of the floor, she screamed at me as if I had broken a precious heirloom or something. 'You always were a destructive little brat!' she said to me. 'I don't deserve this. I've got a terrible headache, and you come in here and destroy my kitchen!'"

I had a hard time with this one. I think it's one of those moments when I gaped at her and asked her to repeat what she had just said.

"You heard me right," she said. "But while she was reading me the riot act and complaining about her headache and how I was making it worse, Chuck came in and was standing right behind her as she skewered me. 'What's going on?' he asked."

I was mentally relieved. The cavalry had arrived!

"So what happened?" I asked.

"So this happened. Chuck raised his hand and said 'Hold it!' 'Connie,' he said to me, 'when you get the children fed, I'm taking you out to dinner. You've earned it. You deserve something a little special tonight.' You can imagine how that sat with herself. She said, 'What about me?' Chuck just looked at her, and said, 'Well, Vicki, since you have such a headache, I think you should eat some soup and go back to bed.'"

"Wow!" I said.

"Wow is right." She had a dreamy look as she recollected that evening. "Chuck took me to this nice restaurant and told me to order whatever I wanted. It was like I was a real person, not a fourteen-year-old girl to be ordered around by her wicked sister and then spat on if I failed to do everything exactly the way she wanted it done."

"What about Chuck's parents?" I had to ask. "Especially when they lived down the street from them. How did they feel about Vicki?"

She shook her head. "I don't know very much, I guess. I was too young to understand everything. But his mother did tell me once that she wished I had married Chuck instead of my sister. I thought she was just being nice, but now that I'm an adult, I understand that she really meant it."

"But Chuck sounds so nice," I said. "How could your sister

be so mean to him?"

Again she shook her head. "Beats me. He was really a great guy. And Vicki treated them all so cruelly. I remember sometimes his mother would call, and Vicki wouldn't let her speak to Chuck. She'd make up excuses why he couldn't come to the phone, and then when she hung up she'd bend double laughing about it. Other times she'd hang up the minute she heard her mother-in-law's voice."

Now I shook my head.

"One of the worst things she ever did," Connie continued, "was when she hung up on Chuck's mother one Christmas Day when she was very ill. When Vicki answered the phone, there was this raspy voice pleading with her not to hang up. Chuck's dad had passed away a month or two earlier, and she had caught an awful cold at the funeral and hadn't got over it. It had probably turned into pneumonia. She wanted Chuck to come over to their house and help her. Vicki just put the phone back on the cradle and said—these are her exact words—'Let the old bitch die!'

"Later in the day, Chuck drove to his mom's home. He didn't know she had tried to phone him, but he did know she was ill and he wanted to check on her. When she didn't answer his knock, he knew something was wrong. He walked around to the back of the house and looked in the kitchen, then in the window of her bedroom. She was lying on the floor by the bed. He broke in through the back door. She was barely breathing. He called 911 and they got her to the hospital, apparently just in time. She did have pneumonia and she was almost dead.

"Chuck never left her side. He called Vicki and told her he was at the hospital with his mom. Of course that didn't sit well. But he must have told her to go jump in the lake, because I know she was mad as hops about it. He stayed there by his mother's side for eight days, until she died.

"He told me once when he had just been through a bitter fight with Vicki that his mother's last words to him as she was dying were, 'Son, get out of your marriage before that woman destroys you. You deserve much better.'"

"What did Vicki say after his mother died?" I asked.

Connie raised her eyebrows and looked at me as if I had asked a foolish question.

"She didn't speak to him for a month. And she gave hell to Mom and me, because she said he had deserted her in her time of need. Get that, will you? *Her* time of need! She was always good at that. Everything revolved around her! She was the center of her universe, and thought she was the center of everybody else's as well."

I learned a lot more as time went by and Connie felt disposed to talk about her sister.

Like the time Vicki got a court order to keep Chuck away from the house because she said he had hurt her. She had been sitting in a chair, she claimed, and suddenly Chuck hit her so hard it knocked the chair over.

The truth, Chuck told Connie, was that he had seen her leaning too far back in the chair and knew it was starting to tip over. So he had leapt forward to stop it, and tripped on a rug as he did so. That threw him into Vicki and they both went over onto the floor.

A LITTLE MORE OF THE STORY

Connie's husband got transferred to New York City, and the family all moved there. I really missed our weekly visits. For a while, we wrote and sent greeting cards, but eventually we sort of lost touch.

Then one day she showed up on our doorstep for a visit. I was overjoyed. It didn't take us long to pick up where we had left off. We laughed and cried and laughed some more. We drank wine and talked until the wee hours of the morning.

I was amazed, in two full days of visiting, that she hadn't once mentioned Vicki and Chuck, but I didn't ask about them. Then, on the third day, she blurted out, "I went to Chuck's funeral last month. You remember Chuck, my brother-in-law?"

"Of course," I said. "How did he die?"

"He was exposed to something in Korea," she said, "and ended up with all sorts of problems, mostly with his lungs. He was in sad shape for two or three years. It was really a blessing when the end came."

"Did he ever get back with Vicki?" I asked.

She smiled. "Yes. They got back together, but he would have been far better off at the end in a hospice or with one of his children. I went to see him shortly before he died. He was bedfast. I sat by his bed and we chatted animatedly about the past. Then he suddenly stopped talking and asked, 'Is *she* in here?' He couldn't see her where she was standing. 'Yes,' I said. 'I don't want to say anything else until she gets out of the room,' he said."

"What did she do?" I asked.

"She huffed out, but not before blaming him for everything bad that ever happened in their marriage. Even as he was dying, she couldn't be civil to him. I watched her go and wondered how in this whole wide world she could have made that fine man's life so completely miserable."

We sat in silence for a moment. Then Connie spoke again.

"Do you have any idea what she had the nerve to say as they lowered his coffin into the ground? She held her handkerchief to her mouth, and in a simpering, self-righteous voice she said,

'I forgive you.' I nearly flipped! What a hypocrite she was!"

Chuck had not been a spineless man. He had done thousands of interviews over the years, some of them with tough, merciless people. But something made him too weak to stand up to that bitch who ruined his life, or at least made it a whole lot less pleasant than it might have been.

"I hope Chuck is dancing with the angels," said Connie, hoisting a glass of wine as if toasting him, "and that they are praising him for how well he dances, even if he sometimes stumbles over his own big feet!"

AN AFTERWORD

I think about the husbands in all these stories. Even though I either knew the people involved or knew the people who told their stories, I still have to shake my head at the thought of so many fine men who let their wives terrorize them. It seems unbelievable!

What is it about some men and the women they love? What strange deficiency in their make-up causes them to renounce their own powers and personalities within the marital relationship? They were all successful in their work, and, presumably, in their social lives outside their marriages. What was there about the marriage relationship itself that rendered them helpless before the women who despised and abused them?

As the mother of such a man myself, I want to shake all of them in behalf of the mothers who have suffered over them and say, "What do you think you are doing?! Wake up and look at what you're allowing to happen! You are squandering your precious lives and deeply affecting other people who love you by being so spineless and cowardly before these terrible women you married. Why do you do it? Don't you really care about your lives and the lives of your other loved ones? Divorce is an easy option today. Half of all marriages end in it. Why do you remain faithful to someone who abuses you and robs you of your manhood? Why don't you simply get out and find a normal life again?!"

Maybe our PC world has something to do with it. Men today grow up in a society that worships political correctness, and they may be afraid to do or say anything that would brand them as callous, insensitive, and chauvinistic.

If that's the case, I'd like to say to them, "Forget PC and give your wives some H and D—that's *hell and damnation*. Remind them that marriage is a partnership, and that you have rights as much as they do. Stand up for those rights, for your larger families if not for yourselves!"

The husbands in this chapter, unfortunately, were all enablers. They empowered their women to treat them abominably. Their very silence and submissiveness allowed their wives to treat them like dogs. No, not like dogs. Some of those wives probably had dogs they treated a lot better than they did their husbands.

The author John Gray might be right, that most men are from Mars and most women are from Venus, because men tend to be rugged and dominant and to exert a kind of superiority over women, who on the whole are more gentle, sensitive, and attentive. But in the sad cases I have been describing, the men's masculinity wasn't enough to counteract the meanness, pettiness, and sheer maliciousness of their wives.

In one of the e-mails I exchanged with our son Richard during the brief time before he went totally off us, I said he was behaving like a wimp. He seemed very offended by this, and asked, rhetorically, "What kind of mother calls her son a wimp?" I wasn't really trying to attack his masculinity, although I'm sure he thought I was. I merely wanted him to stand up for himself when his wife was putting pressure on him to behave in ways contrary to his real nature and upbringing. No parents like to see their sons degraded by strong, ruthless women. We would all like to see them stand up and find the courage to speak for themselves against these controlling vixens.

In Shakespeare's *The Taming of the Shrew*, Katharina had every potential of being like one of the wives described in this chapter. She was self-willed, head-strong, and belligerent. Even in an age when men were the undisputed heads of their households, she wasn't about to be ruled by a man.

But Petruchio, her lover, wasn't having any of her fierce rebelliousness, and set about correcting it. He didn't actually turn her over his knee and spank her the way the hero of the musical *Kiss Me, Kate* did. But he did turn the full power of his personality on her to trump her shrewishness. And in the end they had a wonderful marriage because it was a marvelous conjoining of equals, a meeting of two great, rambunctious spirits!

I wish that our son Richard had the gumption to do what Petruchio did. Maybe only once, for about ten minutes. His whole life would be different if he could only do that. And I'm sure his marriage would turn out stronger and happier for his having done it.

7

ALAS, POOR MR. AND MRS. JOB

The hand of God has touched me. Look at me!
Every hope I ever had,
Every task I put my mind to,
Every work I've ever done
Annulled as though I had not done it.

— Archibald MacLeish, *J.B.*

When we die, and sometimes before, we have
to give up our children and they have to give
us up.

— Rev. Paul Lowder, e-mail to the author

I've been the collector of injustices, the lightning rod of catastrophes.

— Eugene Ionèsco, *The Chairs*

CLOUDLESS SKIES. ROSES WITHOUT thorns. Nights of
unbroken sleep. Flawless gems. Days without pain. Lump-
less pudding. Untarnished friendships. Families that love one
another for life. These are the things of which my dreams are
made.

But they are only my dreams. I have to live with reality.

The parents I have written about in this book have all experienced the joy and excitement of watching their children

grow up to become responsible adults. They've seen a few of their dreams crash as the children have gotten into trouble, failed at school, and generally disappointed expectations. But on the whole they have loved them and cherished them and watched them fondly as they have emerged from infancy to adulthood.

We can only imagine, then, how thoroughly shattered they have been to have the sons in whom they have invested so much love and hope abandon them or even turn on them to appease the whims of the selfish, possessive, unsympathetic wives they have chosen. Shattered...and helpless. Because nobody quite knows how to handle an outcome like that. There wasn't anything in the rule book about it. It always takes the parents by complete surprise.

Knowing what I know now, I can say with confidence that there is one thing all those parents can be grateful for—that they had only one son to treat them so miserably. What if they had had *two* sons in *two* such awful marriages? That's the way it is for Ina and Jack, one of the loveliest, sweetest couples I know.

Ina and Jack were married shortly after the Korean war. They dated through high school and completed two years of college before Jack was called up for duty in the army. When he was discharged, he returned to college and finished a degree in pharmacology while Ina kept house in the small apartment they rented near the campus. Among other things, she repainted all the rooms of the apartment. They worried that she was allergic to the paint fumes because she kept throwing up while she was doing it.

But it turned out she was pregnant with their first son, Gideon.

After Jack's graduation, he joined a pharmaceutical company in Cincinnati, where the three of them—Ina, Jack, and little Gid—settled comfortably into a new house. A year later, a second son was born. His name was Phillip.

Ina and Jack were good parents. They weren't the hovering, demonstrative type, but they were solid, salt-of-the-earth people who transmitted good, solid values to their children. Their sons had the usual childhood diseases, broken bones, and problems at school, but they had happy lives. Both swam like fish, rode horseback like jockeys, and played all the team sports their high school offered. They went to a local university and got good jobs when they finished.

Gid was the more retiring of the two boys. Because of his shyness, he didn't date much, and didn't marry until he was thirty. His wife Laura was a divorcee who worked for the same company that employed him. She had two children from two previous marriages. Gid seemed to enjoy being thrust into parenthood as their step-father, and his parents were delighted to welcome both Laura and her children into their family circle.

It wasn't long before Laura was pregnant with Gid's child. She took her company's generous maternity leave when the child, a little boy, came into the world so she could stay home with him during his first weeks. Even though her two daughters were still young—eight and five—they seemed to be very helpful around the house, and were pleased to have a baby brother.

As her postnatal leave was coming to an end and she hadn't found a suitable nanny for the children, Laura became anxious about having to give up her job. As a last resort, she called Ina and Jack to see if there was any way they could help out until she found a nanny.

Jack and Ina talked it over. Jack had taken early retirement, so there was no problem about work. Finally they agreed to come and stay with the children for a week or two. They thought it would be a happy experience.

What they didn't know because Laura hadn't fully explained the situation was that she was going to work out of town for two weeks, leaving them in complete charge of three children and a household. Gid hadn't yet got the hang of being a father, so from the moment his parents arrived until they went home a month later, they had the full load of custodial duties heaped on them—cleaning, cooking, caring for the girls, and, most importantly, caring for little Barney. They said they had never been more exhausted than they were when they climbed into their car to start home!

Two weeks later, Laura called.

"Can you possibly come back for ten days?" she asked. "I'm being sent overseas for a special meeting. Gid has to go too. So you can see we're really in a bind."

Ina's first inclination was to ask who had been looking after Barney since they left, because she had gotten the definite impression that Laura wasn't much of a mother. But after hearing the desperation in Laura's voice she relented and said they would come.

When they arrived, Gid handed his dad a "to-do" list Laura had typed up for him to follow while they were gone. She assumed that inasmuch as most of the motherly and household duties would fall to Ina, she could enlist Jack to take care of a lot of outside things. She wanted him to repair some gutters that had been damaged by high winds; fix the attic fan, which wasn't turning on and off properly; install some new fire alarms she'd bought; cut down two dead trees in the back yard; chop and stack the wood; paint the inside of the garage; and repair the patio steps.

He couldn't believe it! She was ordering him around like a hired hand!

But Ina didn't get off any easier. There was a typed list for her as well. Laura expected her to polish the silver for a party they were having when they returned; iron the table linens; mend the clothes in a basket by the dryer; purchase matching Christmas sweaters for the children to wear when they had their photo made with Santa; and bake as many cookies and cakes as possible to store in the freezer for their party.

All Ina could say, when she surveyed the list, was, "The nerve of that woman! The very nerve!"

But like the sweet, passive people they were, they both followed Laura's instructions—in addition, of course, to the usual tasks of cooking, cleaning the house, and caring for the three children. The two girls, fortunately, were in school, and little Barney spent much of his time eating and sleeping. So they were able to get a lot of work done.

When Laura and Gid returned—it seemed like ages to Ina and Jack—they had been home less than thirty minutes before Laura said Ina and Jack should be getting their things into the car and heading home so they wouldn't have to be on the roads after dark. Stunned by this rapid dismissal, they assembled their things and left as soon as possible, feeling used and abused by this astonishingly brash and demanding woman.

"I felt like an old milk carton," said Jack. "She took everything I had and then crumpled me up and told me to go home!"

Ina usually called Gid and Laura weekly. Then she noticed that she was doing all the calling. Gid and Laura never phoned. When Gid picked up the phone, he usually gave brief, almost curt, answers to their questions, and almost always in a sort of monotone voice. If Laura answered, she indicated rather quickly that she didn't have time for idle chit-chat.

They hadn't minded calling Ina and Jack when they needed them, but, now that they didn't, they didn't have time to bother with them.

Eight months later, Laura presented Gid with another child, a little girl they named Florence. And, as before, when her maternity leave was almost up, Laura called and asked Ina and Jack to come to the rescue. The nanny they had during most of the pregnancy had left and they hadn't yet found anyone to replace her. Ina and Jack discussed whether they should go. They weren't eager to return and be treated like servants. On the other hand, it was the only way they were going to see their grandchildren. So they gave in and said they would come.

When they arrived, they found another person living in the house, a man named Troy who worked at the same company as Gid and Laura. Introductions were made, but no further information was provided. Ina and Jack wondered why their son and his wife had taken in a boarder, but they assumed it was none of their business so didn't ask any questions.

Having five adults and four children in the house naturally produced some tension. It certainly made more work for Ina and Jack. Troy came and went almost like a ghost, so that he didn't interact with them at all. But Gid and Laura's tempers often seemed shorter than usual. Laura was more critical than they remembered, and once even remarked that they were "more incompetent" than she expected. Gid usually mirrored her attitude, and dropped little remarks about the things his parents didn't manage to get done.

When Ina and Jack had had enough, they decided it was time to go home. On their way, they talked about what they had experienced, and Ina remembered the remark Laura made about their incompetence.

"Yes," said Jack, "Laura is so competent that she can't ever get her clothes on straight. Her blouse is usually half out and buttoned the wrong way. The side seams of her skirts are always crooked. And she might look better if her clothes were pressed. Shame on you, Ina, for not seeing that it was done!"

It helped them to be able to laugh about the way they'd been treated.

But the more serious problem they saw developing had to do with the way their son had taken on Laura's way of criticizing them. They could tell there was a lot of unstated tension between him and Laura. Maybe he was picky with them because he was really angry with her. And they wondered where the mysterious Troy fit into the picture. Did they detect that there was something going on between him and Laura or was that merely overactive imaginations on their part?

A few months later, they got an SOS from Gid. Laura was on a business trip and their new nanny had the flu. Could Ina and Jack please come quickly and stay with them a few days to take over?

Against their better judgment, they went.

The house, they found, was in utter chaos. It looked as if no one had cleaned or straightened it since they were there the last time. Troy, they learned, was on the business trip with Laura—some kind of departmental meeting for their company. And Gid was so busy with his work that he seldom got home before seven or eight in the evening, so that they had the custody of the children entirely to themselves.

They worked hard to turn things around in a brief time and left the day Laura and Troy were to return. They had found their son surly and uncommunicative, as if he had totally taken on his wife's character and didn't really want them there despite his absolute need of their help.

On the way home, Jack shook his head and said, "I don't give that marriage long, do you?"

Ina looked at him. "No, I don't."

Their instincts had been correct. It was less than four months before Gid phoned them one night to say the marriage was over. Laura was suing him for divorce and wanted the house and everything in it. She also wanted him to pay child support for her four children.

"I guess I've been a sucker," said Gid.

"Why do you say that?" asked Jack.

"Well, you know Troy, who was here when you were here the first time. In the course of all the discussions about this, I found out that Florence is really his and not mine."

"You mean, Laura was having an affair with him right there under your nose?"

"I'm afraid so."

"So is he going to pay for Florence's support?"

There was a pause.

Then Gid said, "No, I agreed to pay for all the kids. I didn't want the hassle of a long, drawn-out divorce. It was easier this way."

That phone call was Ina and Jack's last contact with Gid for six years. During that long period, he never phoned them or answered their calls and letters. Later, they would learn that he was in intensive therapy during those years and having a hard time putting his life back together. His relationship with Laura had almost destroyed him. He told them it was all he could do to get to work each day, then stop by his counselor's office before returning to his apartment for a long, lonely evening.

Now, years later, Gid still struggles with his demons from those years. He has seen his children—only one of whom, Barney, was really his—only once since his and Laura's divorce, and they are all now in their twenties. Ina and Jack haven't seen any of them since the last time they babysat for them.

Laura married the live-in friend and they had two children before she divorced him. Gid said there should be a club of Laura's ex-husbands so they could compare notes and decide which child belonged to whom.

As for Ina and Jack, they are thankful for a workable, though not ideal, relationship with Gid. But they have never gotten over the loss of the one grandchild who was really theirs.

THE SECOND SON

Meanwhile, there was Phillip, their other son.

Phillip, or Phil as they usually called him, always reminded his parents of Curious George, the little boy who had to investigate everything to see how it worked. He was always setting things in motion around him.

"He isn't a destructive child," his mother once remarked. "But when he walks into a room, things automatically begin crashing down around him!"

Phil was a happy-go-lucky child. A good student, he also knew how to charm his teachers. He was well liked by all his classmates, especially the girls. He wasn't shy like his brother. He started dating Dana in the eighth grade, when she invited him to be her date for a Valentine's Day sock hop. By the time Phil went to college, they had agreed to marry, and Phil came home every weekend to see her.

Their wedding took place after Dana finished college. Phil's relatives came from far and wide, and everybody fell in love with Dana. "They're the perfect couple," was what Ina and Jack heard from everybody.

But somehow things didn't work out the way they might have in a fairy tale. Phil became immersed in his salesman's job and had to do a lot of traveling. Dana taught second grade and also had a busy schedule. They seldom saw each other. On weekends, they played catch-up on the household chores.

Sunday dinners were always with her folks. After a while, though, Dana started using them as a forum for criticizing Phil. "Phil's never home when I need him." "Phil never gets his chores done." "Phil works hard but he doesn't make a lot of money." "Phil's almost never home, and when he is he's on the phone to his parents." Even Dana's parents were embarrassed at her way of constantly riding him. "Maybe if you and Phil had a baby," her mother suggested, "you wouldn't be so lonely when he's away."

Dana had already thought of that. Phil would surely stay home more if they had a baby. And then he wouldn't waste their precious time phoning his parents. Moreover, a baby would be the perfect excuse not to go visit his parents and spend holidays with them.

Little Francine was born a year later.

At first she consumed all Dana's time and energy. Dana was happy in her maternal role, because it seemed to give her a new purpose in life. She resigned from teaching at the end of the term so she could spend her time with Francine.

Fifteen months later, Nicole was born. This meant looking for a larger house, as the one they were in was already getting small with Francine. Phil wasn't making enough to cover the cost of a larger property, so he began looking around for a new job. The best offer he received was from a company in another state. This worried him, because he couldn't imagine Dana moving away from the town where her parents lived.

But Dana surprised him. She liked the idea of a move.

They found a new home that delighted both of them. It had a small creek in the back, and the girls were happy about that.

Even little Nicole liked to play "splashy-splashy" at the edge of it. Dana seemed happier than she had ever been. "Who stole my babies?!" she would tease the girls about how fast they were growing up. She didn't even complain any more about Phil's parents. She seemed to enjoy their visits, and loved for them to see how much the girls had changed each time they came.

When Francine was in first grade and Nicole was in pre-school, though, Dana began feeling lonely when they were away, and started talking about going back to work. She asked Phil if it was okay with him, and when he said yes she let him know she had already found and accepted a job in a local finance company.

This was when their lives began to change, said Ina. Breakfasts were eaten on the run. A sitter picked up the girls in the afternoons and stayed until Dana got home. Then Dana would throw some frozen TV dinners into the oven, change her clothes, and fuss at the girls to put up their toys so she could walk through the den. The kitchen sink was always full of dirty dishes and the table invariably had splotches of cereal, milk, and orange juice on it.

Phil decided it was time for a family talk. First, he tried to explain to his daughters that they needed to help Mommy keep the house clean. He made a chart with pictures to remind each girl of what her chores were. Then he suggested to Dana that they hire a part time housekeeper.

"I wouldn't need a housekeeper if you carried your weight around here," Dana replied somewhat heatedly. "What are *your* designated duties? I work too, you know. Yet I'm expected to take care of everything while you do nothing to help."

Phil was shocked. He had never seen Dana like this. He had unwittingly released some kind of fury in her.

"Why don't you ask your beloved parents to come and help

us?" she asked. "Goodness knows, they do enough for Gid and Laura. Surely they can lower themselves to help us. I need some relief from all this!"

"Wow," thought Phil. "And maybe from me!"

Phil didn't know what his parents could do, living half way across the state, but he did think it was time for a visit from them, and phoned them the next day to come and stay a few days.

Jack and Ina had no idea what was going on with Phil and Dana. They had always thought of them as their children without problems. Ina had even said to a friend of hers that she wished Phil and Dana could give lessons to Gid and Laura on how to behave toward their parents.

The girls ran madly to greet their grandparents when they arrived, and Phil and Dana were right behind them. Jack and Ina felt like royalty, their coming was so obviously triumphant. But that evening, both Phil and Dana unloaded on them and told them how far behind they were in taking care of household chores. They wondered if the parents felt like pitching in while they were there and giving them a little relief.

Ina and Jack were delighted. So the next day, after Jack took the little girls to school, they rolled up their sleeves and tackled the house. There were lots of little things for Jack to do while Ina cleaned. He replaced plates on some light switches where they were missing, patched a hole in the bathroom where there had been water damage to the ceiling, rented a steamer and cleaned the carpets that had been stained by the pets, and cleaned up some oil patches in the garage.

The kitchen was the most glaring need. Ina and Jack stared at it in dismay. How did anybody ever accumulate so many old TV dinner trays? How did they find anything in the cabinets, they were such a mess? When was the last time somebody scrubbed the countertops and the tile floor?

In a day or two, they had the whole house looking like a new one, and there was a huge pile of discarded materials placed by the street for the trash pickup. They even spent a day shopping for groceries, and restocked the cabinets with soups, canned vegetables, coffee, tea, and cereals.

"At least now my grandbabies won't starve," said Ina to Jack.

Unfortunately, Dana felt threatened by what Phil's parents had done and was not at all appreciative. At night, she attacked Phil when they were preparing for bed, and told him she didn't like the way his folks had taken over her house. "They act like it's theirs," she said. "Why, today they even went out and bought groceries and stocked the cupboard with things they like!"

Ina and Jack could hear the raised voices in the room across the hall, but didn't know what they were saying. They didn't dream it could be about them, so the next day they went back to work and spent another day cleaning and straightening. Ina tackled the closets and Jack tried to put some order back into the shelves in the basement.

That afternoon, Ina felt too tired to start a big supper, so she got Jack to order in pizzas for everybody. When Dana came in from work, she found a festive tablecloth on the dining table and a wine bottle with a candle in it. The children were excited when they thought of it as a party, but Dana was sullen and said little throughout the evening.

That is, she said little until she got Phil in their bedroom.

Again that night, Ina and Jack heard voices as they argued. As Phil would one day report her tirade to his parents, she said such things as "They want us to feel indebted to them" and "I get so tired of their acting like they are better than we are." He also said she accused them of trying to break up their marriage "the way they did Laura and Gid's." Phil said he thought she would have a stroke, she was so upset.

The next day was Saturday, and Dana took command of her house, ordering Ina and Jack to do the things she directed. Among Jack's jobs for the day was to affix some redwood planters she had bought to the rails of the deck on the back of the house.

Jack looked at the planters and told her they were too heavy for the rails, that they would eventually cause the rails to collapse.

Dana lost her temper and, incredibly, began kicking Jack in the shins. He backed away, mystified, and when she approached him again he pushed on her shoulders to keep her at a distance.

"Take your disgusting wife," she shouted, "and get off my property!"

Then she went tearing into the house, crying as she went.

Ina, who was coming through the hallway as Dana came in, reached out and caught her, asking, "What's wrong, child? What's wrong?"

Dana collapsed in her arms. She was blubbering so badly that Ina held her and stroked her as she would a small child. Then she led her into the kitchen and made her a pot of tea.

As Dana got control of herself again, she began talking nonstop. She said she and Phil didn't get along any more and she wanted out of the marriage. She rehearsed Phil's faults, and said he wasn't the man she had married. She said he didn't make enough money and wasn't providing well for them. She didn't really feel anything for him any more, she said, and she resented the fact that he was always trying to get their daughters to love him more than they loved her.

"You didn't raise him right," she accused Ina. "If he had gotten out from under you, we wouldn't be in this mess. You think no woman is good enough for your sons. You broke up Gid's marriage and now you're trying to break up ours. I hope you're happy!"

Ina fought to keep her composure. In a calm voice, she asked if it was possible that Dana was involved with another man.

The question shocked Dana. Then she gave a puzzling answer: "If you asked me if there *is* another man, I'd have to say no. But if you asked me if there *could* be another man, I'd have to say yes."

Ina didn't probe, but she had a pretty good idea that there was someone else involved in Dana's unhappiness with Phil and his parents.

That evening after everyone had gone to bed, Ina and Jack huddled together on the floor of their walk-in closet to talk quietly about all that had transpired. Jack rubbed his shins and said they still hurt. Ina reported everything Dana had said to her.

"Okay," said Jack. "Let's take the girls to school in the morning and then let's go on home."

Weeks passed without word from Phil or Dana. Jack and Ina knew it wasn't a case of no news is good news. In fact, they felt this was quite the opposite. But they didn't want to interfere with Phil and Dana's situation any more than they had wanted to sort out Gid and Laura's. These couples had to solve their own problems.

Dana, like Laura, filed for divorce. And Phil, like Gid, lost everything, including all the tools in his workshop. The male friend Dana had been seeing for the last two years loved woodworking, and he planned to move into the house as soon as Phil moved out.

Somehow Dana managed to brainwash Phil into thinking his parents were responsible for their troubles, so for several years Phil rarely got in touch with them. They only heard from Dana a couple of times, on both occasions because the girls had special expenses such as orthodontics or summer camp and she wanted them to pick up the tab.

OVER THE CLIFF

I know how hard it has been for my husband and me to deal with one son who turned against us because it suited his wife. I find it incredible that Ina and Jack should have been able to withstand this kind of abusive treatment from two sons and remain sane.

The sons have managed to survive, though not glowingly. Gid had a live-in girl friend for a while, and so did Phil. Phil eventually remarried and appeared to be happy, according to Ina and Jack, who confessed that they rarely see either son unless he needs a loan or something else the parents can provide.

Ina and Jack's hearts haven't mended completely, but they have managed to survive. When they speak of their grandchildren, which isn't very often, they always have a wistful look in their eyes. They are still baffled by the way their sons became estranged from them.

"Somehow," said Ina, "it's as if they weren't really our sons at all. I mean, I know I had them and we raised them. We gave them everything we could, and we thought we were a close and loving family. I still remember those wonderful summer vacations when we went to the mountains or the seashore and all had a great time together. But since all the things have happened to our relationship and they've grown so distant, I sometimes lie awake in the night and think, 'They must have been aliens or something. Real children don't behave that way toward their parents.'"

I remember my husband's plaintive words to our son

Richard in an e-mail he sent him regarding some arrangements for his and Monica's wedding. It had already been established that we wouldn't be attending, but we had paid a deposit on the restaurant for the rehearsal dinner and had addressed and stamped a couple of hundred invitations to it. My husband wanted to say we would pay for the dinner, but they might like to change restaurants, and that perhaps they would prefer that we not be the ones to send the invitations. His first words were:

> *We rarely seem to have an hour that isn't shadowed by thoughts of what has happened. We'll probably always wonder why you decided to push the wagon over the cliff and not look down to see if anybody was hurt.*

I am still moved by the melancholy of those simple statements, and I wonder why some sons and daughters-in-law think they have the right to put the sons' parents through such grief and sadness. How will they feel years later if their own children and their children's spouses do the same thing to them?

And how did Ina and Jack bear to have it happen to them not once, but twice? My hat is off to them. I don't know how they've managed to hold on to their sanity after a lifetime of dealing with what they've had to deal with. They've been over the cliff twice!

8

DAUGHTERS-IN-LAW

> Tell me, why are beautiful flowers so poisonous, and the most beautiful the most deadly?
>
> — August Strindberg, *The Ghost Sonata*

> Being an adult is dirty work. But someone has to do it.
>
> — Robert Fulghum, *It Was on Fire When I Lay Down on It*

> DAUGHTER-IN-LAW (Sarah Jessica Parker): What is so great about you guys?
> MOTHER (Diane Keaton): Nothing. It's—it's just that we're all we've got.
>
> — Michael Landon film, *The Family Stone*

AT OUR FAVORITE BED-AND-BREAKFAST in Niagara-on-the-Lake, Ontario, where we go each summer for the Shaw Festival Theatre, my husband learned that the distinguished gentleman across the table from us was a noted psychiatrist and that his wife, a couple of places down the table, was a child psychologist.

"I'm sorry," my husband said. "I hate to do this at the breakfast table, but I'd like to ask a question about something we've been going through with our son."

He hadn't said more than three or four sentences before the psychiatrist interrupted him.

"It's your daughter-in-law," he said.

"Pardon?"

"He's right," chimed in the man's wife. "It's your daughter-in-law."

My husband looked startled that they had come to that conclusion so quickly.

"It's almost always the daughter-in-law," said the psychiatrist. "We have the same problem in our family."

GOOD DAUGHTERS-IN-LAW

Of course all daughters-in-law aren't difficult. Many are wonderful. I have friends whose daughters-in-law are as dear to them as their sons, and who treat them as if they were the queen mother. I myself even have an ex-daughter-in-law who is wonderful. We e-mail one another almost daily, even though she and our son divorced more than 20 years ago. She's a dear, dear person, and we discuss all kinds of things that are going on in our lives.

I have tried to love each of my daughters-in-law, because I think it's important for parents to give their children a lot of slack to build their own lives and to encourage them in whatever they do. I have sincerely wanted our sons to have the same kind of marital relationships their father and I have enjoyed. Each time our sons have married, I have wanted to incorporate their wives into the family so that we could all be like the happy family in Norman Rockwell's Thanksgiving painting.

In my fantasies, I dream of having a daughter-in-law as a

dear friend who wants to go to lunch or see a movie together. Maybe the two of us could go on occasional trips, or just go shopping regularly for the fun of it.

My neighbor Jean has a mother-in-law she does these things with. Not long ago, they went to Disney World for a week, rode all the rides and saw all the shows and had a roaring good time. They ate at ethnic restaurants and laughed and told stories and shared high times together. And they came home telling funny tales about what Ginny, the mother-in-law, did when she got a little tipsy.

That's the kind of relationship I've always dreamed of—one that's built of love and trust and fun and mutual endearment.

Mother-in-laws have always gotten bad press. I know some of it is justified. I hear stories about some mother-in-laws that curl my hair. They are the ones that provide the stuff of jokes and movies like that one in which Jane Fonda played a terrible mother-in-law. What was it called, *Monster-in-Law*?

But we don't all deserve that kind of branding. I know a lot of good mothers-in-law. Several of them usually take their daughter-in-law's side against their own son. They praise their daughters-in-law for their ability, encourage them when they're feeling low, help them when they need support, and give them reassuring comments about what they're wearing or how their new hairdos become them. In short, they treat them as if they were their own daughters.

I like what the French call mothers-in-law. *Belle-meres*. It literally means "beautiful mothers." None of that "in-law" stuff. Just beautiful mothers.

I don't know what the French for daughters-in-law is. Maybe it's *belle-filles*, or "beautiful daughters." It ought to be. It would set a high mark for every daughter-in-law to live up to. And, again, it would rid us of that awful "in-law" terminology.

Belle-filles, I am sure, would recognize from the outset that many of the things they love most about their husbands actually derive from their husbands' parents, and that those husbands wouldn't be the same men if they hadn't been loved, cradled, and trained in the homes from which they came.

"I don't dislike you because you are your son's parents," our son Eric's wife Pia has said. "That would be foolish. He is the man he is because of you. If I disliked you, it would be tantamount to saying, 'I cannot stand my husband.'"

Many young women, I believe, are happy to become part of their husbands' families. Even if they don't fully adore their in-laws as another set of parents who have their best interest at heart, they can at least become friends who have a healthy respect for one another.

Nevertheless, I encounter stories about daughter-in-law problems almost everywhere I turn––in churches, at the beauty parlor, at the post office, at the grocery store, and in neighborhood gatherings. What I typically hear are remarks like this one, which happens to be from a psychologist friend: "I can say anything I like to my own daughter, but I have to walk on eggshells around my daughter-in-law. She takes umbrage at the slightest thing, even if it wasn't intended to offend her in the least."

I had this problem with my estranged daughter-in-law Monica. Even though I was careful from the beginning to try to please her and create a relationship between us, she became angry or resentful at the most absurd things. I never could please her about the hours or days when I invited them for lunch or dinner, regardless of how accommodating I tried to be. Nothing we ever gave her seemed to delight her in the least, and she didn't bother hiding her displeasure. And there was that absurd thing about my asking Richard what she'd like to eat, back when I was preparing whole meals for them that would help her to avoid the allergy problem she had in feeding little Abby, and how she hated it that I had asked him instead of her, even though she wasn't available when I needed to know.

I can understand how a girl would be intimidated or hesitant around her mother-in-law for a while. I was around mine, even though she was a very sweet-natured woman who never behaved moodily or unkindly toward anyone. There is always a kind of unspoken rivalry between two women who both love the same man, albeit that one is his mother and the other his wife. And every daughter-in-law recognizes that her husband's mother was *the* woman in his life for many years. She bore him, bathed him, nursed him, rocked him, told him nursery rhymes, taught him his ABCs, bought his first clothes, baked his birthday cakes, and generally oversaw his life until he was nearly grown. Why wouldn't something in a wife envy this woman all of this and worry that her husband might love her more than he does a wife?

But it is obvious that some daughters-in-law, beyond all this reasonable rivalry, really dislike their mothers-in-law almost to the point of hating of despising them.

COMMON COMPLAINTS

On an Internet website called "The Society of Tortured Daughters-in-Law," I read the complaint of one young woman that her mother-in-law attempted to enter her home without being invited and that after she physically ejected her, the mother-in-law reported her to the police for assault.

Another woman complained that her mother-in-law responded to an e-mail in which she had named their unborn son by concluding, in her own e-mail, "My love to you and Baby —

———," using the wrong spelling of the baby's name, whatever it was. The name was actually the father-in-law's middle name, and the woman's husband had discovered on his own birth certificate a different spelling of the father's name, so they were using that. The mother-in-law simply didn't know it. Her daughter-in-law accused her of "always playing these little subtle games to send out barbs to me."

Another complained that her mother-in-law wanted a copy of a nice photograph she had of her and her husband, but that she didn't want her to have it because she wanted to have the only copy.

"These mothers-in-law," said yet another "tortured" daughter-in-law, "are simply incapable of being happy for their sons. They are losing control, and they hate it. They blame us for taking their son's attention away from them and for taking away an object they can try to control. Seeing their sons grow up reminds them that they are getting older, and they worry they will no longer be useful."

There is probably a grain of truth in these complaints. But it is also obvious that the daughters-in-law who made them were straining at gnats and swallowing some pretty big camels. In my experience, most mothers of sons are at least minimally more mature than the daughters-in-law who complain about them, and the daughters-in-law, being younger and obliged to respect their husbands' parents, should exert more effort to get along with them.

The British Psychological Society's London Conference of 1999 published a major report on mother-in-law/daughter-in-law problems in the United Kingdom. It lists the three most frequently cited reasons for daughters-in-law not liking their mothers-in-law:

(1) *Their mothers-in-law ignored or denied their profes-sional status outside the home.*

(2) *Their mothers-in-law often spoiled their sons and ex-pected them to do the same.*

(3) *Their mothers-in-law had unrealistic expectations of them regarding the performance of domestic duties.*

The report found that "the mothers-in-law generally had no idea what they were doing wrong and genuinely wanted to forge a good relationship with their daughters-in-law."

Sadly, though, the report concluded, psychologists were "pessimistic" about there ever being a genuine improvement in the mother-in-law/daughter-in-law relationship overall, as it appears to be an age-old problem that does not improve with educational advantages, societal changes, or psychological understanding. Some mothers-in-law are really threatened by the loss of their children, and daughters-in-law are usually too young and immature to relate properly to their mothers-in-law.

As I said, I can understand why a daughter-in-law feels envious of her mother-in-law because of the long relationship she has had with the daughter-in-law's husband. But why can't a woman surmount such envy and understand that it would be better for everybody concerned, including her husband, if she got along well with the mother-in-law? After all, her mother-in-law has every reason to be her best friend and ally. They both care about the same man, only in different ways, and if she desires his happiness, she should know that he is more likely to be happy when the two most important women in his life are in a friendly, productive relationship.

I have tried desperately to see our situation from my daughter-in-law's point of view. I too was a daughter-in-law. My husband was virtually an only child—his only sibling had been killed in an accident when he was twelve—and was very dear to his mother. Yet I managed to get along well with my mother-in-law. I encouraged my husband to take her to lunch alone from time to time, so they could talk mother-and-son talk if they wanted to. I always saw that he remembered her birthday and Mother's Day with appropriate gifts and expressions of care. She told me shortly before she died that she had always quietly resented my taking her son away from her at an early age (we married on his nineteenth birthday). But we had a happy, workable relationship for many years, in spite of any secret feelings to the contrary.

REASONS FOR POOR RELATIONSHIP

As I have studied the subject of mothers-in-law and daughters-in-law, I have concluded that the list of reasons they don't get along better is much longer and more complicated than might be indicated by the British Psychological Society's report. Here are some of the things I think are often responsible for the poor relationships where they exist:

FEMINIST ATTITUDES. A number of mothers I have talked with believe that the rise of feminism has had a lot to do with the way their sons' wives have behaved toward them. "It's what they learn in school," said one woman. "They think they're better than the women of our generation."

I confess that I am something of a feminist myself. At least I believe women should receive equal pay for their work, enjoy equal protection under the law, and have equal opportunities in the work place to become whatever they want to be, whether it's doctors, CEOs, lawyers, astronauts, political leaders, or anything else. But I also agree with the women who said to me that they think feminism is like a virus in the educational and communication systems today—that is, in both the schools and the media—so that young women grow up with a kind of narcissism, believing that *their* happiness, *their* welfare, and *their* wishes are more important than those of men. Women grow up feeling that they are entitled to extra consideration and reward as payment for the many centuries in which their mothers and grandmothers didn't have them.

Betty, a friend of mine, has a daughter-in-law who heads an attorneys' office for the U.S. Government. Betty says the girl is intoxicated by her abilities and achievements, although they are actually quite modest. She is always reminding people that she is the first person from her family to graduate from college, and that she has a law degree as well. "Sometimes I want to throttle her," says Betty. "You can't imagine the airs she puts on around us. Our son is every bit as smart as she is, but she acts as if he doesn't know half what she does. My husband calls her 'Miss KIA' behind her back. That stands for 'Miss Know-It-All!'"

A mutual friend told Betty she thought it was "all those feminist courses" in college that ruined her daughter-in-law, and Betty agreed. "Maybe if we had taken some of those courses when we went to college," she laughs, "we'd boss our husbands around and dislike our mothers-in-law too!"

LEARNED PREJUDICE. A close friend of ours who is a paralegal in her mid-thirties tells us that when she was a child of ten her mother had already started teaching her to despise her future mother-in-law. Her mother had had a bad marriage and blamed her mother-in-law for it, so she wanted to prepare her daughter by instilling a hostile attitude in her from the outset.

"Don't trust a mother-in-law for anything," she told her daughter from that tender age. "She'll betray you every time!"

"I have taught my own daughters to do the opposite," said our friend. "After all, I wouldn't even have a husband if it weren't for his mother."

Society has unfortunately done its best to do just what our friend's mother tried to do for her. The portrait of the mother-in-law as a mean, grasping older woman is as old as the writings of Geoffrey Chaucer in the late Middle Ages. Comedians love to do shticks about their mothers-in-law because they always draw big laughs from the audience. I have even heard ministers tell mother-in-law jokes from the pulpit. So we have to admit that learned prejudice contributes a lot toward disrespect for mothers-in-laws in modern society.

SELF-DOUBT AND SELF-DENIGRATION. Some daughters-in-law actually come off badly in comparison with their mothers-in-law, even though the latter are almost always much older and presumably less glamorous. Take Margo, for example. Margo was a very heavy young woman I knew. Her own aunt described her in her wedding dress as looking like "an overweight marshmallow floating down the aisle."

I know her new mother-in-law wasn't thrilled that their son was marrying such an overweight girl, but she managed not to say anything about it. "If our son loves her," she told her husband, "that's good enough for me."

But even before the wedding Margo got it into her head that her future mother-in-law didn't like her and therefore set herself against the mother-in-law. For the entire seven years of her marriage, she has resisted friendly overtures from the mother-in-law. She writes angry notes to her about her husband's faults and about her dislike of the mother-in-law's telephoning to talk to the grandchildren in the evening. She has steadfastly refused to send greeting cards or presents to her in-laws on special occasions, and has taken offense whenever her husband has done so over her protests.

She says her reason for feeling this way is that his mother has always disliked her because she's fat. "She's a bigoted snob," Margo says, "and I'll never like her."

This isn't just a mother-in-law/daughter-in-law thing. Many people don't give others a chance because they feel awkward or ill at ease around them and imagine that others are looking down on them. But it is obviously one reason a lot of daughters-in-law, especially the less attractive or intelligent ones, determine to dislike their husbands' mothers.

INABILITY TO HANDLE NEW RELATIONSHIPS. Some daughters-in-law are simply shy and introverted, and cannot accept or develop new relationships with anybody. Incapable of easy and spontaneous relationships, they are particularly guarded and self-protective against their husband's larger families, even though the families exhibit all the signs of wanting to be friendly and accepting.

One young woman who falls into this category says, "I married my husband, not his family. I don't see why I should put myself out to ingratiate myself with the others."

Jennifer, a girl I met in one of my husband's parishes, was bright enough, but her confidence level was so low that it totally panicked her to be in any kind of group she hadn't known since her days at school. When she and Bill were courting at college, she refused to accompany him to visit his family. Their first exposure to her, other than what Bill had told them, was on the day of their wedding rehearsal. And even then she was taciturn and withdrawn, granting them only an occasional half-smile and very little conversation.

She didn't dislike her new in-laws. She simply became catatonic around them. Her in-laws felt an incipient pity for the girl, but no amount of praise and encouragement on their part seemed to change the way she was. She even went to a counselor for several months after she and Bill married, hoping to be more outgoing and friendly, but it changed her very little.

As Bill's father said to my husband, "I think there's a wonderful person somewhere inside her, but I doubt if we live long enough for her to feel comfortable around us."

Rhoda, a young friend of mine, is a lot like Jennifer. A poor girl, she grew up being tormented by peers because she had a lisp and didn't have the money for nice clothes like the other girls. Turning inward, she spent most of her spare time reading and playing the piano.

When she married Derek, she feared that his parents would see what a shallow, empty person she was, so she tried to avoid them as much as possible. Derek's mother said she reminded her of a small, scared child hiding behind her mother's skirt. When they visited the parents, she wouldn't ever stay in a room if Derek wasn't there too. He became the shield she hid behind when she was with her in-laws.

The in-laws are respectful of Rhoda's feelings. They still have hopes that she will someday overcome her insecurity and accept the embrace of a family that wants to love her. It will be a miracle, they say, but that is what they're praying for.

JEALOUSY. It is no accident that jealousy has always been considered one of the seven deadly sins. Its effects can be strongly poisonous, not only to the jealous person but to others around that person as well.

I'm thinking of a girl named Emily, whose parents are

friends of ours. Her mother says Emily has always shown a streak of jealousy, ever since she was small. They tried to help her grow beyond it, but as she grew older it only seemed to get worse. When she was in high school, her mother talked with a school counselor about it, because Emily's jealousy of some of her classmates was taking all the joy out of her life.

After Emily married, her jealousy became a big problem for her husband Ray. If he spoke to another woman, even when Emily was present, he was always in for a period of sulkiness or recrimination. When he worked late at the office during tax season—he was an accountant—Emily was sure he was conducting an affair. She was always pelting him with questions about who he saw during the coffee break, who he had lunch with, whether his mother called him at work, what she said if she called, and whether she talked about Emily.

She was particularly jealous of Ray's mother Janine, who was a tall, dark-headed, attractive woman and had once been a photographer's model. Emily despised Janine because she was clever, articulate, and had a sunny, upbeat disposition. She imagined that Ray was always comparing her to Janine and finding her lacking in some quality his mother had.

"I can't stand your mother," she would complain. "She isn't nice to me. She doesn't answer a lot of the e-mails I send her. She just drives around in that big car of hers like she owns the town. I know she looks down on my family and me. I can't understand why you ever want to see her again."

It was a shock to Janine when she discovered the depth of Emily's jealousy and hatred for her. It came out one evening when the family was sitting around a patio table having coffee after a barbecue dinner. Apropos of nothing that had been said, Emily suddenly spat at Janine, "If you were gray-headed, short, and dumpy, I might consider liking you!"

There was an awkward pause after this outburst. Ray's father looked stunned. Ray was embarrassed. Janine was the one who broke the ice. "Well, I'm sorry I'm not like you, dear," she said as sweetly as she could. "Maybe in the next life." Then, to relieve the situation, she got up, stacked some empty cups and saucers, and carried them into the house.

After that, Ray came around less and less frequently. Janine knew it was because of the way Emily felt. She was disappointed in her son, but knew he had to pay a price if he was too friendly with his family. It was more important to her that her son be happy and that his marriage should survive than that she got to see him as often as she once did. If the marriage failed, she didn't want to be the one responsible for it.

GREED AND SELFISHNESS. In a sense and to a degree, we are all selfish. Even saints have been known to cherish things for themselves, such as time and space and individuality. So it isn't a wonder that it is also a problem in some mother-in-law/daughter-in-law relationships.

I know a woman named Michelle who declares unequivocally, "My son married the most selfish girl on the whole planet!" And, after hearing her story, I don't think I would argue with her judgment.

Her son Jim owns a small picture-framing shop. He loves his work, and enjoys the freedom of taking as few or as many jobs as he pleases. He meets the public well. He often plays classical music during working hours at his shop. What he does suits his personality beautifully.

Joanie, Jim's wife, has a high-pressure government job. She leaves their house at seven in the morning and doesn't get home until eight at night, and is on call at any time. A career woman of the first order, she has zealously worked her way up the promotions ladder. And the more money she makes, the more she salts away in an account that has her name on it, not Jim's.

"'Me' and 'mine' are all she ever dreams or talks about," says Michelle. "If Jim ever complains that she's spending too much time at her job, she tells him he's the one who has all the problems in their marriage, not her. She says, 'If you were only a little more ambitious, I could relax and not work so hard.'"

Michelle says she has always been very kind to Joanie, but secretly agrees with her son that she has her priorities screwed around. She thinks Joanie is shortchanging him in the marriage and doesn't appreciate how patient and tolerant he is.

One night after dinner, Joanie forgot herself and unloaded on Michelle. "She had had three glasses of wine," said Michelle, "and didn't know what she was telling me. She said Jim wasn't earning enough to suit her. He was a dreamer, she said, and she couldn't stand his sunny optimism about everything. That's why she was putting her money into accounts with only her name on them, and living on the money he made at the shop."

"Then," said Michelle, "after a fourth glass of wine, she turned to me and said, 'When are you and Ben gonna kick the bucket and leave everything to us?'"

"No!" I said. "Surely I didn't hear that right."

She nodded. "I know. I thought I didn't hear her right either. But when she saw how shocked I was, she tried to make a joke of it. I knew she wasn't joking. She'd like nothing better than to get her hands on everything we have."

"But you said she makes a big salary herself," I expostulated.

"Yeah, she does. But nothing's ever enough for her. She wants a bigger house and a Mercedes and a lot of things they don't have. I used to think it was all a pose, just a lot of raw, naked ambition. But now I don't think so. I've known her long enough to know she means it. She'd really like to inherit all we have and use it as a base for going on to an even bigger fortune."

I laughed, trying to ease the obvious tension Michelle was feeling. "You need a food taster," I said.

"Darn right," she laughed. But it was only half-funny, given what she'd just said.

Psychologists say that half the fights in any marriage are probably over money or what it can buy. I have known enough women who were spendthrifts to believe that. Some men spend a lot of money too. But in the cases I've known, it's five to two the women are the ones who're exhausting the bank account and running up credit card debts.

So personal greed and selfishness are a heavy mark against joy and happiness in marriage, and mothers-in-law are probably right when they say they hate to see these qualities in their daughters-in-law. No matter how hard their sons work, or how much money they make, it will most likely not be enough for some of their wives.

A SENSE OF SUPERIORITY. This is usually the mirror-reflection of a sense of inferiority, but that makes it no less a problem. Some daughters-in-law enter marriage with a sense of smugness about their own backgrounds, especially if they have been more fortunate economically or educationally than their new in-laws. And it often happens that those who come from backgrounds clearly inferior to those of their husbands get a kind of reverse sense of triumph out of the fact that they have managed to climb above their previous stations and marry into wealth or status. Either way, it presents a difficult psychological situation for daughters-in-law and their husbands' parents.

My friend Margaret has a daughter-in-law who came from what Margaret calls "the wrong side of the tracks," but her poor and deprived background never really mattered to Margaret and her family. In fact, they appear proud that Lucy managed to get an education in spite of certain handicaps and then secure employment as a stenographer in the large corporation where their son Alton was a vice president.

After their marriage, Alton and Lucy bought a lovely brick home in a fashionable suburb, she stopped working, and they started a family. Lucy was justly proud of her home. It had several acres of lawn, a tennis court, and a three-car garage—all symbols to her of wealth and status. And as children came along, a maid and a nanny were employed. Eventually there were four children, and the family added a large den, a studio, another bathroom, and a beautiful sunroom to the house.

For a while, Lucy seemed to thrive under her new circumstances. She divided her time among several clubs, including a tennis club and a golf club, and earned a reputation as a contributor of both time and money to civic and political organizations. She had more than she had ever dreamed of having, and truly flourished. She felt superior, and liked the feeling.

In her evolution from a poor young bride into a wealthy doyenne, Lucy gradually eliminated her husband's family from their lives and elevated her own family. His parents felt a definite chilliness when they visited, but her own parents eventually moved in with her. Her husband's siblings were as unwelcome as his parents, but she saw that hers were all aided financially.

"We were always a very close family when Alton was growing up," Margaret remembers with a note of sadness in her voice. "But now, I don't know, it's as if someone dropped a couple of stitches while knitting a sweater and the hole in the finished product will never be filled in."

Religious differences. Our society is generally more ecumenical than it was a few years ago, so that most people are respectful of other people's religious beliefs and affiliations. But this isn't true for everybody. Some people who are raised in a particular faith grow up thinking it is the only faith worth having and find it difficult to accept persons of a different persuasion.

Take Wilma, for example. Wilma was raised in a home where church-going wasn't encouraged. In her teens, she began attending an evangelical church where a particular youth leader made her feel personally important. Soon she joined that church and became an avid supporter of its programs.

When she met Mark and fell in love, she soon persuaded him to attend her church and become a member there. When they married and had children, the children were baptized into that church.

But Wilma was troubled by the fact that Mark's parents and siblings, who lived in another town, belonged to the Episcopal church, whose approach to worship and life was much less evangelical than her own. She didn't feel right about trying to proselytize them, but neither did she feel comfortable going to their church when she and Mark visited them. She complained to Mark that it was "cold" and "lacking in the true gospel."

At first, this disparity didn't appear to matter very much. But as Mark and Wilma's children grew up, she became increasingly critical of his family's faith and often labeled it "apostate" or "heretical." She was particularly insistent that her children should always belong to an evangelical church and never consider joining a church like their paternal grandparents' church.

Mark, who was not a religious zealot, tended to overlook his wife's passion for evangelicalism. But he finally saw that Wilma's attitude was coloring their relationship with his parents more and more, even to the point of her not wanting to take the children to visit them. He didn't openly oppose or criticize her position, as he wanted to maintain a peaceful relationship with her. So he mostly drifted along, permitting the chasm between his present family and his former one to become wider and wider.

My husband and I aren't certain, but we strongly suspect that our problems with our son Richard and his wife Monica stem at least partially from the fact that she is from a Roman Catholic background and has always felt strange or embarrassed that her father-in-law is a well-known Protestant minister and that Richard's background was Protestant as well. We had no anxiety about his marrying a Catholic, and she never said anything overtly about his being Protestant, but we believe her family wasn't comfortable with their earlier plan to have my husband perform their wedding ceremony and that that might be one reason they decided not to let him do it.

We believe our grandchildren have all been baptized into the Catholic Church, probably on various trips to visit Monica's mother in Florida, where she is very supportive of a particular priest. Monica is too ritualistic to have allowed them to remain unbaptized. But no word was ever breathed to us about the baptisms, and we saw no photographs of them, although the family is very big on picture-taking. Richard himself has remained mum on the subject. That side of his marriage was never brought up, even when we were communicating with them.

THE NEED TO MANAGE OR CONTROL. Some people grow up with an innate need to be in charge of others. This leads to their becoming university administrators, corporate leaders, city executives, military officers, or political figures. And even if they don't achieve recognizable positions in society, they try to exercise dominance in their own households and family operations.

For centuries, of course, women had little opportunity to manage their own destinies. Legally regarded as chattel owned by their husbands, they had limited spheres of operation and only those in charge of large households, with maids and servants, could truly fulfill their inner need to rule over others. Some women naturally dominated their husbands, certainly; but in public they were required to appear meek and submissive.

Today, when women enjoy much more equality, there is little in societal structures to inhibit the full exercise of any inclination they feel toward management, and even very young girls often experience the thrill of maneuvering males into doing exactly as they want. Girls even joke about it among themselves, and plan devilish things to order the boys to do so they can laugh at them when they do them.

When young women accustomed to managerial techniques marry, they frequently regard their husbands' mothers as obstacles to their total control over their husbands, so set out immediately to nullify the mothers' influence. As they are in charge of their own households, they have a real advantage over their mothers-in-law, and sometimes exert it to turn sons against their mothers.

A realtor friend recently described a situation in the lives of two of her clients, Cal and Mimi, whom she was assisting in finding a new house. As she had been working with them two or three months and had had several lunches with them, she knew a lot about them.

Mimi, she said, obviously wore the pants in her family. She and Cal had been together five years and had had a child two years ago. Now Mimi had decided it was time for them to get married and move into a house of her choosing. "Whenever there's any difference of opinion about a house I show them," said my friend, "I always know whose opinion will count. If Cal says he doesn't like something, Mimi tells him what they can do to change it or work around it. If she doesn't like it, on the other hand, they're out of there in a flash!"

My friend had also got to know Cal's parents, Sam and Margie, who were expected to help pay for the new house and had therefore gone along to look at a couple of favorites. Sam had strongly advised against buying one of the houses because he said the builder had cut corners and used substandard materials in places where it didn't show. Mimi had become very frosty toward him after that, and, when the parents weren't within hearing distance, had made some catty remarks about them.

"I could tell," said my friend, "that there's no love lost between Mimi and her in-laws. Sam and Margie are the sort of people who are in charge of their lives, and don't like it that Cal knuckles under to her on everything. Apparently she tells him what to wear, what to do, and what to think, and he sort of says, 'Yes, ma'am,' and does it. So she tries to keep him away from his folks as much as possible in order to minimize their influence."

"I have to laugh," she continued, "when I think that Mimi has to put up with them right now until she gets the money out of them for the house she wants. I think it's killing her!"

JUST PLAIN MEANNESS. My husband, who is something of a theologian, has often remarked that John Calvin, the doughty old Reformer, was correct when he said, in effect, "People are no damn good." From the beginning of time, there have been some people who simply can't get along with others. And there are a lot of daughters-in-law who fall in this category. They make everybody miserable because they're simply mean, ornery people.

My friends Jordan and Tess are absolutely afraid of their daughter-in-law, Mottie. Their son Jordan Jr., whom they call Jordy, is also afraid of her. They all knew she was difficult before her marriage to Jordy, but Jordy said at the time that she was only under stress and would be fine once the wedding was out of the way. He thought he could handle her little temper squalls.

But within a few months of the wedding, everybody began to see a spiteful side of her that couldn't be explained away by stress. She was just plain mean! As Jordan said in a voice reminiscent of Colonel Potter on the old *M*A*S*H* programs, "She's ornerier than a bobcat with a wasp up its behind!"

Jordan and Tess could tell when things started going really badly between her and Jordy. So they tried to think of things the four of them could do together that Mottie might like, hoping it would soften her attitude toward all of them. They took her and Jordy with them on trips to the seashore, the mountains, and even overseas.

Jordan said he wouldn't ever forget their first day in France. Mottie got mad at them because she didn't get the room she wanted overlooking the courtyard of the hotel they were staying in––the one he and Tess were assigned—and started shunning them. When they went to a museum, she would spot them and hustle Jordy off in the opposite direction. Occasionally they would see their son and daughter-in-law coming down the street ahead of them. Then Mottie would see them and steer Jordy off down a side street so they wouldn't meet.

"And to beat it all," said Jordan, "when we went to dinner in a fancy restaurant, she rewarded us by sitting sideways at the table so that she looked out into the room and not at us. I felt like putting her across my knee and giving her a darned good spanking, but I had to restrain myself for our son's sake!"

Eventually Mottie got tired of even the nice trips her in-laws took her on, and all but forbade Jordy to see them or have anything more to do with them.

Shaking his head, Jordan said, "That girl has been nothing but cruel to us. She does weird things sometimes, like calling us ten or twenty times a day and not answering when we pick up the phone. We know it's her calling, but she's just trying to bedevil us. We've even seen her drive her car into our driveway and sit there without coming in, then drive away. We decided our son married a crazy woman!"

"You should read the threatening letters she wrote us," said Tess. "Things like 'You won't see your precious son again' or 'I know how to rig car bombs.' One time she came up on our porch, threw a bucket of red paint on everything, and rang the bell. When Jordan saw what she had done and she started to swing the rest of the bucket at him, he ducked back inside and slammed the door so he didn't get hit by it."

"How does Jordy stand it?" I asked.

"Blamed if we know," said Jordan. "I'd go stark, raving mad if I lived with that woman."

"We know she's mean to him," said Tess. "He didn't tell us himself, but a friend told us one time she locked him out of the house and he had to sleep in the car."

I could only shake my head in sympathy. Their daughter-in-law sounded like a real sociopath to me. But she isn't the only one I've heard about.

A TEST FOR PROSPECTIVE DAUGHTERS-IN-LAW?

Having a daughter-in-law today can be an awful business, and I have to admit I don't know how some of the situations I've described can ever be resolved. I sometimes think little boys should be trained, from the time they can walk and talk, to take up for themselves in this increasingly female-controlled society. They need to have it instilled in them that they have the same rights as girls.

That also goes for in-laws. We have rights and feelings that should be respected by these cute little girls who grow up to be our monster daughters-in-law.

Like most ministers, priests, and rabbis, my husband required couples planning to marry to have counseling sessions before he would perform their service. He always asked them questions about religion, finances, life goals, personality types, ambitions, dreams they had about having a family, and how they functioned in their former families. Sometimes, when he spotted potential problems the couples would face, he talked to them about these. Once or twice he tried to dissuade them from marrying.

Such sessions are helpful, especially if the participants are honest and forthcoming about themselves. But from my point of view, it would be wonderful if there were a battery of questions that could be administered to all prospective daughters-in-law. There are tests for virtually everything these days—entering school, getting a driver's license, becoming a therapist, a police officer, a school teacher, even working at Wal-mart. Why shouldn't there be a test for daughters-in-law who are going to become part of our families and may very well threaten to interrupt everything we have always treasured?

Here are some of the questions I would propose to have on such a test:

1. Describe typical interactions between your mother and father. Which one usually wins an argument? Are they fair in resolving conflicts?

2. *How have your parents treated you? Have you been hurt or abused by either or both of them? If so, how have you handled your relationship to them?*

3. *What kind of family do you and your husband want to have? Will one of you be the boss? If so, which one, and why?*

4. *What is your idea of shared responsibility in a home?*

5. *Do you like to discuss issues and get to the root of them? What kind of discussions have you been accustomed to in your family?*

6. *Do you have strong religious or moral concerns? What are some of them? How do you see them affecting your relationship with your husband?*

7. *Which women are your heroes? Why?*

8. *Do you think mothers-in-law are usually a problem? Why or why not?*

9. *Do you like the idea of sharing birthdays and holidays with your husband's family? How do you feel about sharing them with your own family?*

10. *What problems do you anticipate from your in-laws? How do you think you would resolve them?*

If a prospective daughter-in-law were willing to submit to such questions, and answer them honestly and seriously, her response might become the basis of a real learning experience for the whole family. Perhaps a marriage counselor or psychologist could be invited to sit in on the discussions and use them as a launching pad for further discussions.

It has often been said that communication is the key to all

relationships, including marriage. If that is so, then anything we can do to promote better and more complete communication between husbands and wives and their families is important— even before the marriage takes place.

But this only works when the husbands and wives are willing to communicate, and my son Richard and his wife Monica have not been. For the first time in our son's entire life, we haven't been able to discuss a problem we have. The very first time. So I can only conclude that our daughter-in-law, for whatever reason, will not permit it.

9

HOSTAGES OF THE HEART

There is no more beautiful witness to the
beauty of the word made flesh than a baby's
naked body.

— Madeleine L'Engle, *A Circle of Quiet*

That in itself—snuggled with my grandchildren—was gift enough.

— Marilyn Brown Oden, *Hospitality of
the Heart*

Would Arnold's children feel deprived when
they grew up? As if they were part of nothing?

— Maisie Mosco, *Glittering Harvest*

It is a good thing to have one's grandchildren around
you when you have finished working. You can see the
results of all your hard work then.

— Alexander McCall Smith, *The Miracle at
Speedy Motors*

THERE IS A WONDERFUL LITTLE interlude in Anne Tyler's
Breathing Lessons in which Maggie and her husband Ira
are going to a funeral and stop at a rural snack bar on the way.
Maggie takes up instantly with the waitress, a woman named
Mabel, and they soon begin talking about their children.

Maggie tells Mabel about their son Bobby, his wife Fiona,
and their "darling little baby"—how they were living at her and
her husband's place because they didn't have very much money,

how there was an argument, and how Fiona took the grandchildren and moved out, totally crushing Maggie.

"Grandbabies," says Mabel. "Don't get me started."

Grandchildren give older folks a *raison d'être*. They make us forget our problems and infirmities. They are the hope of the future. My mother used to say, in her elder years, "I could sit on the side of the bed every morning and rehearse my aches and pains, but they're not going to ruin my day." The reason she said that was that she had ten grandchildren whom she adored. She couldn't wait to get up and see who might come by to see her that day. Life was good because of the children!

I didn't realize at the time how fortunate my mother was that all her sons and daughters came home and shared their children with her. Now, after what we've been through with Richard and Monica, and after listening to dozens of other couples who've had similar experiences, I know it might have been otherwise. Some daughters-in-law don't like to share their children with their in-laws, and will do almost anything to prevent its happening.

It's sad.

I think about a beautiful lavender cyclamen I had. The older it grew, so that the stems were ragged and awkward looking, the more the blossoms multiplied and the greater became their translucence and beauty. I imagine what it would have been like to pinch off those gorgeous blossoms and leave only the ugly stems. That wouldn't make sense at all. And yet it's exactly the way I see my life without grandchildren. I grow older and less attractive all the time, and don't have my beautiful grandchildren to justify it.

In our case, there's an added dimension of hurt and insult. Monica has taken an unusual interest in my sister, whom she has never seen, and often sends her packets of photographs of her babies. My sister tells me about it on the phone, and seems to enjoy being the object of such attention. I don't usually say anything, but I feel as if there's a dagger in my heart and it is being slowly twisted. It's bad enough that my husband and I don't get to see our grandchildren and don't receive their photographs. But it's fiendish of Monica to send these photo troves to my sister, because she knows it increases my sense of agony at not seeing them.

A COMMON STORY

A lot of grandparents tell me they have similar problems. One said she could never count on seeing her dear little granddaughter. If she and her husband made plans for a special outing with the little girl, the girl's mother would cancel them at the last minute and then tell the little girl, "Well, Grandma finked out on you again!"

The maternal grandmother, on the other hand, got to keep the little girl as often as she liked.

Last Christmas, this particular grandmother and her husband were given an hour at their son and daughter-in-law's home to open presents with the grandchildren. Then the children were bundled up and taken away to the daughter-in-law's parents for the rest of the day.

"It's unjust," commented this grandmother. "But there's nothing we can do about it. And we can't say too much or we'll lose the few privileges we have now."

Our son and his family spend holidays with our daughter-in-law's relatives. Before we became estranged, we were given glimpses of our grandchildren at *early* Christmas parties or *early* birthday suppers, never on the actual dates, which were reserved for her family. And even then Monica was always poised for instant flight. The minute she wasn't the center of attention or had ceased to enjoy herself, she would tug at Richard's sleeve and say, "Come on, we've got to be going!"

The last time our son and his family had a meal with us was two days before his forty-second birthday. We knew there would be a big celebration at their home and her parents and brother would be there, but we wouldn't be invited to that. I spent most of two days preparing a special meal, complete with a big birthday cake, and we had bought and wrapped several gifts for our son. Our other son and his wife were there too. We had barely finished the meal and Richard hadn't quite opened the last presents when his wife said they had to leave because there was somewhere she needed to go.

Our time was over.

One man wrote on the Internet that his wife is a wonderful wife, mother, mother-in-law, and grandmother, but has the same issues with her daughter-in-law that a lot of us suffer. "There is no earthly reason," he said, "that she should be treated that way."

"We have to fight for a tiny amount of time with our grandchildren," he continued, "and it hurts us when the other grandparents get to be with them any time they want to."

Their daughter-in-law, he added, is petty, vengeful, and puts words in their mouths that they've never said. He wished their son would get involved in the situation and try to secure some justice for them, but he plays it safe and lets his parents go on suffering humiliation and loss.

I sympathized with the man when I read his complaint, because it is an almost universal story among grandparents whose daughters-in-law are insensitive to their needs and desires. When we grow older, it is the little ones who renew our faith in humanity itself, in the ongoing of the human race and the perdurance of life when we are gone. To be deprived of that reassurance in a kind and meaningful way is—well, it's an unkind and unjustifiable fate.

I sometimes wonder what our son and his wife will think and feel some day if one of their children—and it only takes one—turns on them and treats them the way they have treated us. I try not to wish it on them, because it's best not to be vengeful. But sometimes I can't help wondering.

GRANDPARENT CARETAKERS

It is ironic that some of us have the problem of not seeing our grandchildren in an age when a lot of grandparents are charged with the more or less full time task of taking care of theirs.

The last time I looked up *grandchildren* on Google, there were more than 25 million entries, at least 99 percent of which referred to grandparents who were taking care of their grandchildren most of the time while parents worked, traveled, or pursued personal interests. Many entries offered advice about how to feed the grandchildren, how to educate them, how to entertain them, how to give them a sense of family and rootedness, what to do with them on trips, and how to raise them with love and tenderness.

How I wish!

A lot of grandparents today get to raise a second family because their children are divorced or both parents are working. Some even complain that they didn't choose to raise another family when theirs was grown, and feel that it's an imposition on them to be pressed into service a second time. I'm sorry for you, folks, but to me that would be grandparent heaven!

I remember a time before our second granddaughter was born—the one we barely saw before Humpty fell off the wall—when our daughter-in-law Monica said she was thinking about going back to work as a teacher and wondered if I might be available to come and stay with our first granddaughter two or three days a week. I was ecstatic! I could see the two of us having fun for hours. We would play games, watch videos, slide down the slide, swing on the swing set, take walks, play in the park, laugh, sing, and be as happy as two little puppies all day long! I felt younger and peppier than I had in years. There was so much to look forward to!

But Monica got pregnant again and there was no more mention of her going back to work. I secretly hoped, though. I thought, maybe she'll want to do it after this next baby is a year old. Then, alas, came our estrangement, and I realized my dream could never come true.

Now Monica has had her fourth child, according to my sister. My dream was only a pipe dream, and now I realize it. My heart aches for what might have been.

AN EPIDEMIC OF SADNESS

My husband remembers a woman in his New England parish who complained that her son had been very close to her until he married, and then his wife made it more and more difficult for them to see one another. She nagged him to move away from the community where they lived, even though his job was there, and relocate in a township several miles away.

When they had a baby girl, the grandmother hoped it would bring them all together again, but it had the opposite effect. The wife was always having her parents visit, but never his. When the woman called to see if she might come to visit even for part of a day, her son's wife always had something else to do.

Once, when a meeting had been arranged, the mother took a bus to the children's town and walked from the bus stop to their home. When she rang the doorbell, no one answered. She waited around for almost an hour, hoping her daughter-in-law had run to the store or something and would be back, but she didn't return. So the woman went back home feeling sad and depressed. She said she never received a word of apology or explanation. It was just the way things were.

The woman was often on the verge of tears when she came to see my husband, and usually gave in to them after saying a few sentences. He felt sorry for her, but did not know that one day he and I would be in the same position with our own grandchildren.

In another church, my husband had frequent visits from a woman who was tearful because she couldn't see her little grandson. When the boy was born, his mother allowed the grandmother to help with the baby and household chores. She got to hold the baby, bathe him, change his diapers, and attend him much of the time. Naturally she fell in love with the little fellow.

But when the child was about a year old, the mother decided he was getting too attached to his grandmother. So she limited the woman's visits to half an hour a week. Then, after a few weeks, she said she couldn't come around any more unless she and her husband invited her.

The grandmother was devastated. Some days she thought she would go crazy if she didn't get to see her grandson. Those were usually the days she came to see my husband, and he said she would sit in his office wiping away tears and looking as if her heart would break.

My husband had another parishioner who had a similar grief. When her grandson was a few weeks old, the mother walked away and left him with his father. The father had to work, so he asked his mother to keep the child during the day. A widow, she had no other demands on her time, so she suggested that she move in with her son and the child to look after both of them. The son was delighted, and she did.

Then a couple of years later the son remarried. His mother lost no time finding a small apartment nearby, so she could continue to care for her grandson, because the son's new wife had a job and couldn't care for him herself.

But the new wife turned out to be quarrelsome and undependable. She didn't like her job or the people she worked with. It wasn't long before she began oversleeping and going in late. Within a couple of weeks, she was fired. At that point she decided to take over the rearing of her stepson. So she notified the grandmother that she must stop coming to the house unless she was asked to come. And the invitations became less and less frequent.

The grandmother was heartbroken. She loved her little grandson more than anyone else in the world. When she couldn't see him, she became depressed, and my husband worried that she might even be suicidal. He tried to encourage her by suggesting that maybe the son's wife might not stay with him or might decide to take another job. He also told her to think about the possibility that when the child was older he might seek her out on his own and the two could be great friends.

"When the grandchildren are grown," people say to me, "they will find you." People mean well. They think this is helpful. But my secret thought is always this: "What about all the wasted years between now and then?"

I expect the woman my husband counseled thought the same thing.

Friends of ours had a son who walked away from home when he was in his teens, and they had no idea what happened to him. As the years passed, they wondered if he was all right, if he was married, if he had children. Twenty-seven years later, he appeared at their door and asked if he could come home.

Most of us grandparents don't have 27 years to wait for our sons and their families to return to us. And suppose our estranged grandchildren did come to visit us when we're older. Wouldn't it be like meeting total strangers? What would we say to one another? How would we mourn the passing of the years?

WHO GETS THE SHORT STRAW?

One thing is certain. If one set of parents gets the short straw, it will be the husband's, not the wife's. I've never known it to happen otherwise.

I can understand why it's this way. It's normal for a daughter-in-law to turn to her parents for help with her children. She has spent all her life with them, and she feels comfortable raising her children in their presence. And she simply doesn't stop to think how her husband's parents probably feel when they are ignored or shoved aside.

Sally and Ned live fifteen minutes from their grandchildren, and they eat, breathe, and sleep those children. They think they are the brightest, most gifted, and most adventurous grandchildren ever born. But they don't get to see them often because their daughter-in-law Amy calls the shots and decides when and if they can visit. They often feel hurt at being left out of holiday dinners and birthday parties.

Sally confesses to me that she gets angry about it, then vows each time that she won't, that she will rise above it all.

"But it doesn't work," she says. "I can't stop thinking about my grandchildren and wondering what they're doing. I can't win with Amy for losing. If I said I didn't care and didn't want to see them, she'd accuse me of not loving them. Yet when I tell her I would love to see them more often, she acts as if I'm trying to take over. What's wrong with her anyway?"

I suppose it could be worse. What about mothers who turn their children against the grandparents by constantly saying unkind or untrue things about them? Some mothers actually do this, and create an air of hostility and rejection that the grandparents can never overcome.

My friend's sister Alice systematically brainwashed her children to despise their paternal grandmother. When they were small, she refused to take them to their grandparents' home and wouldn't allow the grandparents in hers. She always told her children that Grandma was an evil woman who would find some way to harm them, like the witch in the Hansel and Gretel story. The children grew up believing that Grandma should have been institutionalized.

And all the while their grandmother couldn't understand why she wasn't allowed to visit the children. Her son never stood up for her, even though he knew what a gentle, kind woman she was and that nothing his wife told the children was really true.

Whenever he saw his mother, which was usually for a brief time and in secret, his mantra was, "You know Amy, Mom. It's easier for me to go with the tide. But I love you."

His mother died without ever really getting to know her grandchildren. And the saddest thing is that those children never knew what a wonderful, loving grandmother they had—

or might have had, if their mother hadn't been such a selfish, insensitive woman.

Speaking of Amy and of a mother dying without knowing her grandchildren reminds me of a column called "Ask Amy" that appeared in *The Washington Post* for July 20, 2005. It contained this letter from a man who signed himself "Tortured in Vancouver":

> Dear Amy:
> I have unbearable guilt.
> I am a 49-year-old, educated, successful man. I was raised in a loving home with three siblings.
> My parents were attentive, hardworking, and in love with each other. My mother went to work outside our home so that we could have college money. We were all loved and cared for unconditionally.
> I met and married a difficult woman. She is selfish and spoiled.
> From the start, she made it clear that she wanted nothing to do with my family, so we moved 3,000 miles away. To keep peace with my wife, I have ignored my parents and siblings for 25 years.
> Over the years my mother sent us countless letters, cards and gifts. All her time, money and efforts went unacknowledged. I did not send the photos of my children she begged for. My life was easier that way.
> My mother died this week. There is no funeral or memorial service for me to attend.
> Because of me, my children will never know the grandmother they deserved to have.
> I can hardly stand to look at myself in the mirror. I cry all the time. My wife is aloof and calls me a hypocrite.
> Now, I am compelled to see my father and siblings, but I am afraid they will run me out of town, and who could blame them?

Should I chance it and show up? My wife is against it.
How do I live with such guilt?

If I had been answering that letter, I would have said "How,
indeed?!"

ANOTHER TRAGIC CASE

Jean, a very special friend of ours, lost two sons to Hodgkin's
disease. She is a wonderful woman, and one of the most mag-
nificent examples of courage, love, truth, beauty, and faith I have
ever known. Her husband died while he was still relatively
young. Then, a couple of years later, she lost the two boys.

After the death of her son Doug, his wife, who lived in a
small house that belonged to Jean, compounded her grief by
dropping all contact with her. She no longer permitted Jean to
see her grandchildren, whom she dearly loved. She also sued
Jean in an unsuccessful effort to wrest the house from her.

Once, several years later, Jean ran into one of the children,
a teenage girl, on the street. She realized it was awkward for the
girl, who had been told God knows what about her, but she
cherished the opportunity for a brief visit. It was the only time
she was able to see any of her grandchildren.

The daughter-in-law finally moved away, and after a long
agony of silence Jean wrote her a Christmas letter suggesting
that they reassess things and see if they couldn't achieve a reconciliation. That letter was subsequently published in the Sara-
sota *Herald Tribune* for January 1, 2006. Jean said she agreed to
its publication because she hoped it might become a model of
reconciliation for others.

"Looking back on these past nine years and our estrangement after Doug's death," she wrote, "right and wrong were balanced against each other. The choice once made had irrevocable results. It has been a growing experience for me as well as a heartache when you and the grandchildren were no longer a part of my life. If you too have regrets, please put the past behind and begin the New Year with a renewed relationship."

My heart ached for Jean because I understood how deeply she desired to be a part of her daughter-in-law and grandchildren's lives again. Apparently her daughter-in-law read the letter, because last Christmas we had a note from Jean saying they were getting together again after all this time!

A HAPPY ENDING

I sometimes hear from grandparents who haven't seen their grandchildren for years and then are approached by them with a request for money or help of some kind. The grandparents' reactions are always the same. First they are grateful and excited that their grandchildren have looked them up after all the years they have missed. Then they are crestfallen when they realize that the children are only after money or physical help of some kind, not familial bonding.

"It's almost like looking at a perfect stranger who has come to your door for a handout," said one grandmother. "You feel hurt and insulted, and wonder if you should pander to them by giving them anything at all."

A grandfather named Jim said that his doorbell rang and he went to answer it. His grandson Pete, whom he hadn't seen in years, was standing there, looking awkward and ill at ease.

Then Pete blurted out his reason for coming. "Grandpa," he said, "I need two hundred dollars for a special pair of athletic shoes. Mama doesn't have the money to give me."

When Jim didn't react quickly enough, Pete continued: "I figure you owe me the shoes to make up for all the birthday and Christmas presents you didn't send me while I was growing up!"

Jim opened the door wide and invited Pete in. He took Pete's coat and laid it on the sofa. Then he led the boy into the basement to show him where he and his wife had stored all the gifts they had bought for him and his brother through the years. All the gifts had been sent through the mail and had been returned to the sender unopened.

Amazed, Pete went through box after box. He couldn't believe how thoughtful his grandparents had been in their choices of their gifts for him and his brother. He loved the funny cards tucked in some of the gifts.

An hour went by, and Pete and his grandparents were still sitting on the basement floor talking, crying, and laughing together.

Pete said, "Grandpa, could I mow your yard for you? I'll mow it as many times as it takes to earn two hundred dollars."

Jim smiled. He reached out his hand, and grandfather and grandson shook to close the deal. When Pete left after sharing some supper with them and talking some more, he didn't hesitate to hug both of his grandparents—his *newfound* grandparents!

Sadly, most grandchild stories don't have such a happy ending.

A SAD FACT

My husband and I were rejected by our son and his wife before our two oldest granddaughters, Abigail and Rachel, could really get to know us. We'll always have wonderful memories of the times we saw them as small children, but unfortunately they were too young to remember us. They will grow up knowing their parents' friends and their various babysitters and the maid who works for their mother—and of course their maternal grandparents—but not us.

We live only a few miles away. I think of them every day and wonder what they're doing and how tall they are and how animated they are about all the things going on in their young lives. A few months ago, my sister told me Monica said she had had little Abigail's long red hair cut for the summer and they took the hair to a center where wigs are made for children who have lost their hair in the process of undergoing chemotherapy. I've thought of little else for days, and wished I could see her and could have been a part of her excitement about that. I grieve for what I'm missing of her life.

Each Christmas, someone in my family sends me Richard and Monica's Christmas card with the picture of them and their children on it. I always tape it up onto the refrigerator door, where I look at it a dozen times a day. Last year there were three little ones on the card. This year there were four. Little Brian hadn't been there before. I felt very strange seeing him for the first time in a photograph sent to me by a third party.

Little Abigail always looks like my husband's pictures when he was a boy. Her sister Rachel looks like my husband's Aunt Lulu when she was a child many years ago in Idaho. Our daughter-in-law Monica never liked it when I mentioned the resemblances. She appeared to like it even less when I gave her a photograph of Aunt Lulu when she was small. It was obvious that she didn't want her children to look like my husband's side of the family.

That's tough, because they always will.

It hurts to see those beautiful children and not be part of their lives as they are growing up. I try to pretend I've gotten over them, but obviously I haven't. What did Eugenia Price say in her book *Getting Through the Night*—"Memories may be the whetstone that brings to grief its sharpest edge."

How true that is! I wish I could forget I've ever known those precious children, but I can't.

On a recent walk with my husband I admitted to him how much I was missing them.

"Oh honey," he said, "you'll always miss them. It's as if that whole part of our family—our son, his wife, and those beautiful grandchildren—were all wiped out in a terrible car wreck. You can't ever forget a thing like that!"

I thought of a friend in Birmingham, Alabama, who lost her husband and only daughter in a collision, and how she must have felt when a police officer came to her door to give her the awful tidings. We went to see her a few hours later, and found her so devastated she could barely talk. I imagine that even now, after several years, she remembers that awful experience and has to put her hand to her heart to try to still it.

"That's true," I answered my husband. "I'll never get over it."

Mabel was right about what she said in *Breathing Lessons*. "Grandbabies—don't get me started!"

10

An Elegy for What Might Have Been

"What is wrong with the cows?"
I ask my approaching neighbor.
"Oh, they've taken their babies away,"
He explains matter of factly.
"So they're sad, you see."

"Taken away their babies," I repeat,
Catching the sadness
That only a mother can feel.
"To be sold," he answers.

— Phyllis Stump, *Walking the Gunnysack Trail*

That's what makes it so hard—for all of us. We can't forget.

— Eugene O'Neill, *Long Day's Journey into Night*

He woke with a start....He cried out,
My son, my son, my son.

— Alan Paton, *Cry, the Beloved Country*

WHAT ARE THE FAMOUS LINES FROM John Greenleaf Whittier's "Maud Muller," the poem about a judge and a maid who should have married but didn't?

For of all sad words of tongue or pen,
The saddest are these: "It might have been!"

"It might have been." Powerful, heart-wrenching words. There are a lot of reasons parents grieve when their children go their own way and no longer have anything to do with them. One is that they are missing all the wonderful things that might have been a part of their lives and aren't.

All the birthdays, Passovers, Easters, Christmases, and Hanukkahs . . . All the trips they could have taken . . . All the music they might have danced to and the theater they might have seen . . . Going to Disney World . . . Seeing the grandchildren dressed up for Halloween . . . Attending their school programs . . . Special times around the dinner table . . . All the picnics . . . Reminiscing about the past . . . The laughter and the tears . . . Work and play . . . All the things that make life exciting . . . All the memories that could have been . . .

It might have been.

Our son Richard doesn't live in the past any more. We realized that the last time we were together, when we began to reminisce with him and his brother about fun things we did through their lifetimes. He said he couldn't remember. Someone has been tampering with his ability to recall the beautiful moments. That's very sad for him.

A similar thing happened at Christmas a year or two before that. We were having our Christmas dinner a week before Christmas—Monica's decree!—and I asked everyone to think about their favorite Christmas as a child and share it with the rest of the family. Richard couldn't think of anything to tell. That shocked us, for he had always loved Christmas and said it was the best time of the year.

It was as if his past had been annihilated, and there was only the Richard of today, in the present tense. Maybe my husband was right, and Monica has really taken over his inner life as well as his outer life. Something inside him has been exterminated!

Richard is actually a wonderful human being. At least, the son we knew was a great person. He always had a lot of zest for life and knew how to fill each day with joy and excitement. He was a bit of a daredevil, and we sometimes wondered if he would survive childhood. He went at everything with a winner-take-all attitude. He was always in motion, going somewhere, building something, painting a picture, mastering a new dance step, composing a song on the piano, conquering the world, racing toward tomorrow!

I particularly cherish a tender memory of the two of us sitting at the piano when he was eight. I was playing and we were singing. Remembering that beautiful, sweet voice of his brings tears to my eyes as I write this.

I truly miss that son.

It hurts me to think that Monica has managed to kill off that person so she can have the cardboard Richard she has now, who professes not to remember the past and lets himself be pushed and pulled in any direction she wishes.

Even when they were courting, Monica didn't like our talking about him as a boy and young man. She showed us a photo album of her family but didn't want to watch our slides of Richard when he was young. It was almost as if she had already willed that Richard to die, to vanish from the face of the earth, so she could substitute the one she was training, the one she willed him to be.

Now she has fixed it—and he has too—so that she'll never have to listen to anything else about his past. At least not from his parents and his brother. Those days are gone, if she has her way, forever. Humpty-Dumpty has had a great fall.

WHAT OUR GRANDCHILDREN WILL MISS

I find it sad that our grandchildren won't have access to those stories and memories of their dad. They won't ever get to hear about what he was like when he was their age—how feisty he could be, how he got so hyper when he played games that he often cried, how he excelled in everything at school, how he enthralled his friends by dancing and singing, how he always took the lead in plays at school or church, how he became so worked up at the approach of Christmas that he sometimes had to leave the table and throw up his food.

They won't ever hear about the time their father, his brother, and his parents lived in a garret apartment in Paris and their father spent half days in a bilingual play school where most of the children were French. They won't get to laugh at his fierce little announcement when he came home one day, "I not Flinch and I not speak Flinch!"

They won't know what a shock their grandmother got the day she walked into the living room of that apartment and found him sitting on the ledge of an open window, leaning out to look down on the street four stories below, or how coolly I began singing as I moved toward him so I wouldn't frighten him, until I could seize him and pull him out of harm's way.

They won't know that when he was small he sometimes messed up words, like the time he came in the house and complained, "I lost my glubbs in the creep!" Like the way he said "lellow" for "yellow" and called M&Ms "M&Ns". Or like the way he was always mixing up "yesterday" and "tomorrow," so that he would say "I did that tomorrow" or "I'm going to do that yesterday."

As talkative as the grandchildren are, they won't ever know that their dad was extraordinarily loquacious as a child, so that his teacher sometimes made him go into the cloakroom and stop disturbing the other children, or hear about Mrs. Wolf, the other teacher who reported this to us and said she sometimes sat and chatted with him while he was in the cloakroom because she enjoyed him so much.

They won't hear how he started making fancy Christmas tree ornaments when he was still a boy so he could sell them and earn money to buy presents. They'll never see photographs of him in the costumes I made for him when he was in various plays and musicals, or know about the funny poems and stories his grandfather wrote for him to recite in the oratorical contests he won.

However good they are at sports, the grandchildren won't hear what a fierce competitor their dad was—how he hated to lose and would sometimes cry when he lost at Horse or Pony on the basketball court, and broke tennis rackets when playing with his dad because his dad had outfoxed him.

They won't get to laugh about the time when we were living in New York and their dad, at age five, took the scissors and cut a big swath right down the middle of his lovely blond curls, so that he was embarrassed at his own appearance and went down the street with his head tucked under his dad's arm. Or the time, years later, when he went to Florida with some friends on spring break and they all peroxided their hair, only his turned a funny orange color and he wanted me to give him the money to go to the beauty parlor and have it changed back to a more natural color, which I wouldn't do because I said he'd have to live with his mistakes.

Nor will they hear about the time I was driving home from a meeting to be there when their dad got home from college and I saw a disreputable looking young runner on the side of the road with a beard, long hair, a red bandana around his head, a pair of jeans with slits at the knees, and a faded old fleece jacket. "Some poor mother," I thought to myself, "has a son who looks like that!" A moment later I realized who it was and slammed on the brakes. "Omigosh," I said, "that's *my* son!"

How the children would laugh and giggle about all those things!

But unfortunately they're probably never hear any of them, because their dad has renounced his past life in favor of the one Monica wants him to lead now and it is a life largely devoid of humor and idiosyncrasies, one that's homogenized and sanitized to suit her notion of what a nice, sanitized husband ought to be like.

I'm so sorry, because their lives and imaginations would have been far richer if they'd had all these biographical details to understand who their dad really was.

MORE OF WHAT THEY'LL MISS

I wish too that I could share with my grandchildren the experiences my husband and I have had through the years—a lifetime of joy and happiness and adventure that has taken us all over the world.

I'd like them to know how poor we were when we got married and lived on $25 a week my husband was paid as pastor of a small rural church. As the children of a mother who has inherited a fortune, they'd have a hard time believing we bought a five-cent snow cone in the park on Sunday afternoons and shared it with one another because we couldn't afford two, and that I actually fussed at their grandfather one Christmas for paying two dollars for a Christmas tree we really couldn't afford.

I wish I could tell them about our country parishes, and

how those poor people saved their butter and egg money for weeks to buy us our china, crystal, and silver flatware when we got married. I still can't think about those wonderful folks and their generosity without shedding a tear or two.

I'd like to tell them about all their granddad's students who used to come to our home when he was their teacher, and how now they're scattered all over the United States and abroad and still write or call him to say he was the best thing that ever happened in their lives, and about all the important places where he has preached through the years, including the National Cathedral in Washington and Riverside Church in New York and a lot of countries abroad, and about the many books he has published in his lifetime, on subjects as varied as Ernest Hemingway, absurd drama, children's loneliness, Christian spirituality, and Harry Potter.

I grieve that my grandchildren won't know their uncle Eric, who is one of the finest human beings who ever lived and has a mind like a bear trap for everything he ever hears or reads and has contributed numerous brilliant articles to a big, important encyclopedia of psychology, or their aunt Pia, who could tell them about growing up in Serbia and loving books even though she could buy only one a year and coming to this country to make her own way when she was in her early twenties.

Who will ever tell them that I'm descended on my mother's side, the Prathers, from Caesar's praetorian guard, and that their grandfather is descended on his mother's side, the Ellises, from the original owners of Ellis Island in New York harbor? Or that their great-great-grandfather Killinger was a sheriff in the old Wild West, and their great-grandfather Waddle, who became a banker, was honored as the oldest living World War I veteran in the Commonwealth of Kentucky, or that both their great-grandmothers on their father's side were school teachers before they married?

They won't ever hear the hilariously funny stories from our families, such as the one about our Dalmatian named Zeus, whom we left with my parents when we went overseas for a summer. When it was almost time for us to return, my mother put Zeus's mat into her old-fashioned washing machine to have it spotless when we saw it. But the great mass of hairs in the water clogged the hose as the water was running out. As she always did in such cases, my mother put the hose to her mouth to blow it free. When she did, she gathered a great intake of breath to make her compelling exhalation. But in doing so she sucked an enormous hairball into her throat and nearly choked.

Nor will they hear the tale of their great-grandfather Killinger, a large man, who was up on an extension ladder painting his barn near the highway when the ladder slipped and one of the rungs came down on his feet so that he couldn't work them loose. As he wriggled around in the attempt to extricate himself, his pants cascaded down around his ankles, and he still couldn't get loose. Drivers blew their horns, but no one stopped to help. Finally a neighbor lady, hearing all the honking, came out and discovered his plight. By this time in the story we were always laughing so hard that we never did hear how she managed to help!

There are dozens, perhaps hundreds, of stories like this in the family archives, narratives that pop out automatically like blooms on a Christmas cactus, that those precious children will never hear, because their father either doesn't remember them or, in his new identity, has ceased to care about them.

Our grandchildren may be wealthy in material things, but they will be at least partially impoverished because their grandmother didn't get to teach them to play the piano or cook or knit or sew. They will miss their grandfather's teaching them not to be afraid of things, the way he taught Abigail not to be afraid of thunderstorms, or to make a whistle from a blade of grass, the way he taught our sons. They will miss the rich holiday traditions in our household, and fondling all the bits of china and brass and wood we've collected from stalls and art galleries around the world. They will miss our introducing them to our hosts of favorite places, such as the cathedrals of Chartres and Notre Dame, the cliffs at Mendocino, the giant redwoods at Big Sur, the Shaw Festival Theatre at Niagara-on-the-Lake, the bookstores of Greenwich Village, the caves of Tintagel, and the footpaths of the English Lake District.

The children will miss the humor that constantly reverberates through our house—the jokes, puns, witticisms, and stories that often go on for hours at a time. They will miss our sharing our great collection of children's books with them—the ones their father and his brother had—and playing old *Let's Pretend* records their father and uncle loved when they were small. We saved them all for our grandchildren to enjoy. And when they're older they'll miss poking around in our voluminous library, that spills over from their grandfather's study into two small libraries on other floors and enfolds a playroom in the basement!

What they're going to miss is priceless, inestimable, beyond value, and it will all be because their father and mother have chosen it, have sentenced them to miss it without waiting until they were old enough to have a vote in the matter.

Shame on their parents!

WHAT WE SHALL MISS

And what shall my husband and I miss because of this alienation?

We will miss the natural joy of watching our grandchildren grow up.

We will miss the excitement of tracing family similarities in them.

We will miss helping them understand themselves and their parents in a world where everything is in transition and becoming more and more difficult to understand every year.

We will miss getting to introduce them to our cherished religious thoughts and values.

We will miss seeing them get dressed up for their first proms.

We will miss all their graduations, from grade school and middle school and high school and college, and, who knows, maybe even from law school or med school or some other graduate institution.

We will miss hearing about their first romances and watching them blush as they describe their first dates and first kisses—if children ever blush about things any more.

We will miss being able to give them hugs and squeezes and telling them endlessly about how very much we love them.

AND ALL OF US?

What are our son and his wife missing with us?

Celebrations of everything.

Sharing our feelings about life and the children.

Trips we might have taken together.

Seeing our son's first gray hairs and the deepening of the crow's feet around his eyes.

Sharing our talents—our son's art, his wife's management skills, my husband's writing and speaking, my own writing, cooking, decorating, and playing the organ and piano. Our love and laughter and humor. Especially our love.

ECHOS OF THE FUTURE

It saddens me to think how much richer all of our lives would be if we could only share them with one another. The passing on of life and history has been interrupted, and from all the signs it will continue to be. Our son and his wife no longer want his parents, brother, and sister-in-law in their lives. Humpty-Dumpty is no more.

I don't remember who said it—maybe it was Tennyson— but it comes to me from somewhere: "I am a part of all that I have ever met or known." I believe that. None of us live or die to ourselves. We are bound up with all that is. But our grandchildren's lives have been tragically restricted by their parents' actions, so that what they can know of their dad, their uncle and aunt, their grandparents, and all the forebears on our side of the family will always be greatly limited.

Part of their own past has been walled off from them, and, with it, the present and future as well.

In some ways, I think this ranks as a crime against humanity.

The last time our son and his family were in our house— on the occasion of his pre-birthday party—I know I felt an indefinable chill in the air, an omen for the future. Our son was distant and passive, and his wife was aloof. While they said their perfunctory goodbyes, I had a terrible premonition that they would never visit us again.

Bending down, I took Abigail, who was two, in my arms and said, "Give Grammy a hug that will last her for the rest of her life!"

I haven't seen any of the children since. Our lives together came to an end that day. I'll never think of that line from Whittier without remembering them or of them without remembering the line in the poem.

What might have been . . .
       What might have been . . .
              What might have been . . .

11

WHERE DO WE GO FROM HERE?

Were you all havin problems?
We don't have problems. When we have prob-
lems we fix 'em.
Well, you're lucky people.
Yes, we are.

— Cormac McCarthy, *No Country for Old
Men*

Hints, and lesser hints.

— Thomas Klise, *The Last Western*

Don't feel totally, personally, irrevocably responsible for everything. That's my job. Signed, God.

— Jan Karon, *A New Song*

IT'S EASY FOR PERPLEXED PARENTS to get in the habit of
taking the blame for any disruption or unpleasantness in the
family. My husband and I are old hands at this. When we had
tried everything we could think of to persuade our son to talk
to us about what was bothering him and his wife, my husband
wrote them a long letter in which he apologized for everything
he could think of.

They didn't bother to answer.

The more I think about the matter, the more convinced I am that there are many failures involved in the breakdown of a single family.

Society has failed.

Education has failed.

Humanity as a whole has failed.

We have failed.

Our sons and their wives have failed.

Sometimes, it seems, life itself has failed.

In the best of all possible worlds, we would all love and enjoy one another so much that nothing could spoil our relationships and happiness. Children would feel loved and wanted from birth to death. Schools would be great blenders of love and joy and encouragement. Relatives would all join together to make life on earth a paradise for us and our children. Everyone in our community would feel like a natural part of everyone else.

But it isn't the best of all possible worlds and things don't always work that way.

Who am I trying to kid? They *seldom* work that way.

Perhaps we parents are at fault for making our home atmosphere too happy for our children when they're growing up. Then they grow up and marry and don't know how to cope with a different kind of setting. Maybe their spouses weren't raised the same way and are much more adept at fighting for what they want and controlling their territory.

The sum of it is, we parents aren't perfect and the system isn't perfect. There will always be conflicts between daughters-in-law and their husbands' families, and maybe even sons-in-law and their wives' families. And some conflicts will be thornier and harsher than others.

The question is, What do we do? How can we deal with the

situation we have in the most effective, constructive way?

START EARLY

There aren't any easy answers. But maybe we should start by educating our children about what can happen to them when they marry and how they ought to behave when they get into larger, more inclusive families. Girls should be taught that they owe something to their husbands' families as well as their own, and should be drilled in the mantra, "When in doubt, respect!" Boys should be warned that they may marry girls who will instinctively try to put a wedge between them and their families, and trained in how to cope with such situations when they arise.

My husband, who is wise about many things, argues that if sons only knew how to stand up and be courageous, they could do a lot to defuse family problems. They could shelter their wives against overbearing family members, and, in the same manner, take the part of their own families when necessary. After all, they are in a key position to become traffic cops, therapists, mediators, and mature adults in the conflicts arising out of their marriages.

Most of our sons don't know how to do this when they marry. They have grown up in a world where women are respected and it isn't politically correct to dominate them as men once did. This tends to confuse them. They don't want to betray their families of origin, but they don't know how to handle wives who say unkind things about their mothers, fathers, and siblings or begin to shut them out of their lives. Their natural instinct is not to make waves. So they swallow their objections and go along with their wives, sacrificing themselves and their families to whatever the wives want and insist on.

Why shouldn't parents teach their sons from an early age that wives can be like that, and talk about what the sons can do if it happens in their marriages? Perhaps if sons were aware of the possibilities when they get married, they would be prepared to understand and handle their situations more adroitly. How wonderful if they had been taught to say, "Look, dear, let's get this thing out in the open and discuss it so that it doesn't get out of hand and affect our relationship. I love you, but I also love my family, and I expect you to respect that. I won't love you less if we have a good relationship with my family, I'll love you more. Do you understand? I expect you to be a good daughter-in-law to my family and I'll be a good son-in-law to yours."

FOR INSTANCE

Let's take an example. Suppose a son marries a girl who immediately tries to shut out his parents and siblings. This actually happened to Sam and Eileen and their son Thomas. "My daughter-in-law is so difficult," said Eileen. "She has had it in for me from day one. I can't do anything right and I'm tired of trying. Whatever I buy for them ends up at her parents' home. She doesn't want to touch anything I give them. She seems to have so much contempt for me. One time she got really angry with me for giving my grandson a cookie. 'Do you want him to be fat like you?' she said. I don't ever feel comfortable with her, and frankly I think she terrifies Thomas."

Perhaps two things might have forestalled this ugly situation.

First, Eileen might have had a frank talk with her daughter-in-law in Thomas' presence. "You don't have anything to fear from me," she might have said. "There is nothing I want more than for you and Thomas to be happy. I'll try not to interfere with your lives in any way, and if I seem to be infringing on your space, please let me know. But I expect to continue seeing my son, and your child as well. I am entitled to share in at least part of their lives. I want to be your friend, not your enemy. So let's agree that it will be that way and we'll all get along beautifully."

Second, at his mother's prompting, if necessary, Thomas could have stepped in the minute he saw things going sour between his wife and mother. "Look," he might have said to his wife, "I don't like what I'm seeing and hearing here. I'm sure you don't mean it, but you're hurting my mother's feelings. You must try not to do that, because my mother is important to me. I don't do that to your parents, do I? If you mistreat my mother, it's the same as mistreating me. So please be careful what you say and do, and let's all try to be a big, happy family. Okay?"

As I said, this isn't a perfect world and this approach may not always work. I'm not sure it would have worked in my family's situation. But at least it's worth trying.

A LITTLE EDITORIAL ON EDUCATION

It would be helpful if public schools offered more psychological preparation for life. Every high school student ought to learn about family systems and how they work, and about abnormal or disruptive behavior patterns and ways of dealing with them. They learn English, history, languages, social studies, math, geometry, chemistry, physics, biology, art, music, and home economics. Why shouldn't they be given courses in the way human personalities function, and how they themselves can understand and interrelate more effectively with parents, friends, and future mates?

Think what even one basic course in psychology could do toward helping them understand and relate to their parents, get along with peers, fit into society as a whole, and prepare for responsibilities in the adult world.

Biology will always play a primary role in young people's attractions to other persons. But being better prepared to analyze the personality types of those to whom they're drawn might equip them with some very helpful checkpoints on their journey to the altar and provide the basic understanding of interpersonal relationships that would enable them to build sounder and happier marriages.

THE IMPORTANCE OF BEING PREPARED

Even before an estrangement in the family occurs, parents ought to prepare themselves for its possibility. Unfortunately, most of us think nothing like that will ever happen in *our* families. I know my husband and I didn't. If we had realized that it might, perhaps we would have been wiser and more discerning at the beginning and could have done something to avert its worst consequences.

I remember saying to my husband years ago when our friends Brian and Sue had a falling out with their son Jimmy that I couldn't understand what had happened to them. They had been loving, thoughtful parents and had always gotten along beautifully with their children. Then, after Jimmy married, the relationship seemed to disintegrate. I was completely baffled, and recall saying that such a disagreement couldn't happen to our family because our sons were too precious to us and we had always gotten along well with them.

All parents need to understand one thing. It *can* happen to them, regardless of how wonderful their relationship with their children is. Circumstances change, and so do our children when they come up against unexpected obstacles.

If I had only known this before our family fell apart, I think I could have processed everything more easily instead of stumbling blindly from day to day, trying to make things work while dealing with my pain and grief. As it was, I think I went through all the stages of grief that Elisabeth Kubler-Ross spoke about in her classic study *On Death and Dying.*

First, I was shocked and denied what was happening. I couldn't believe what was transpiring. It was like a nightmare, and I wanted to wake up and find out that it wasn't true at all. I thought I must be misreading everything, and that soon our son would relent and come to see us. We had been too close and loving for him to treat us that way for long. I believed he would come to his senses and the world would turn right-side-up again.

After the denial came anger. I was really distressed with Richard and Monica. How could they possibly behave the way they were toward my husband and me? Who did they think they were? I wanted to turn them over my knee and give them both a good spanking! Why should I even want a relationship with a son who had betrayed us the way he had? How could I ever trust him again? And as for Monica, who did she think she was, anyway, waltzing into our family that way and disrupting our peace and tranquility?

Next, predictably, came the bargaining stage. I wanted to negotiate with God, negotiate with our son and his wife, negotiate with anybody and everybody who might be able to restore things to the way they had been, the way I thought they ought to be again. I would swallow my pride, eat crow, do anything. At this point, I was nearly crazy. I felt as if my son were dying

and only I could save him, but I couldn't reach him to help. I
think I would have done almost anything to make things okay
again.

Then I fell into depression. I couldn't sleep well, and would
lie awake at night turning everything over in my mind, replaying
all our exchanges, trying to figure out the next move to make.
During the day, I couldn't concentrate. I would sit and stare for
hours, unaware of the world around me. I lost my appetite.
Nothing seemed to afford any pleasure. My whole life felt as if
it had gone down the toilet. I even had occasional thoughts of
suicide, because if I couldn't get along with my son and his family why should I want to live?

At last, I had to arrive at an acceptance of the facts. I couldn't
go on in the tormented state of mind I was in. It was making
me unhappier than I could remember having ever been. It af-
fected everything I did, everything I said, everything I hoped
for. It was corroding my entire spirit. I could even understand
why a lot of parents divorce after the loss of a child, because if
they became the way I was, nobody would want them around
any more.

Okay, I said to myself, my son and his wife have done this
to us and there is nothing we can do about it. We have desperately tried to mend things with them and they have resolutely
spurned all our attempts. Something is wrong with our son that
I can't change, and I cannot spend the rest of my life mourning
the loss of him. It's time I shaped up and began looking at this
thing for what it is.

That's when I decided to write this book, because by then I
knew that John and I weren't the only parents to whom this had
happened. If I wrote the book, it would not only help other parents facing the same problem but might help me to exorcise the
demons that were driving me to the edge of lunacy.

At this point, one quotation kept running through my mind. It was from Rosamunde Pilcher's novel *The Shell Seekers,* although I'm sure I remembered it more vividly from the film starring Angela Lansbury than I did from the book itself. The mother in the story had lost her husband, a famous artist, and her children were irritated with her because she wouldn't sell all his paintings and divide the proceeds with them. Their selfish behavior was about to drive her mad. At last she summoned up the courage to make her own decisions and, if necessary, live her own life apart from her bickering, rapacious offspring.

"I do not need my children," she declared. "Knowing their faults, recognizing their shortcomings, I love them all, but I do not *need* them."

This saying became my mantra. I repeated it over and over, at all hours of the day and night. "I love my children, but I do not need them." "I love them but I do not need them." That idea, that concept, played a big part in my finally being able to accept what had happened and adapt to the changes in my life.

SOME GOOD ADVICE

One day when I was at this stage of acceptance, my husband and I had lunch with our friends Roy and Kay Woodruff. Roy— *Doctor* Woodruff—was for many years president of the American Association of Pastoral Counselors, an organization of ministers trained to offer psychological therapy in churches, synagogues, and hospitals. Roy and Kay knew about what had transpired with our son Richard and us, so the subject naturally arose in our conversation. After we had chatted about it for a few minutes, my husband asked, "Roy, if you had only one word to say to parents who have gone through what we have gone through with our son, what would you say to them?"

Roy didn't bat an eye, but went straight to the point. Obviously he had faced similar questions numerous times. "Don't try to fix it," he said. "You can't. So accept the situation and try to fix yourselves."

Then he added, after a brief pause, "And be careful not to fall out with one another."

It was the soundest advice we could have had.

I had to admit, at one point in my grief process, that nothing my husband and I could do would change the situation we were in. We simply had to back away from it and give up our son and his family. We were at the bottom of a deep hole and there was no point in digging any further. Humpty-Dumpty had fallen off the wall, and there was no way we were going to put him back together again!

We had wanted desperately to preserve our family the way it was, to maintain that Norman Rockwell idealism of which I've already spoken. But, if only for our own health's sake, we had to stop dreaming about reconciliation. As our son had said that day at the restaurant, it wasn't going to happen.

Of course, any of us who are suffering this kind of division in our families might be the lucky ones whose son, like the Prodigal Son in the Bible, comes back after a number of years or whose grandchildren seek out their grandparents and want a relationship in spite of their parents. But we have to be reconciled to the fact that it may never happen. The hole in our hearts may never be mended. Life is what happens, and we can't go on expecting everything to work out the way we wanted it to.

Joshua David Stone, in his book *Soul Psychology*, offers this wise counsel: "Choose to look at the other person's behavior," he says—in this case, our children's unkindness—"as being your master teacher, instructing you in a lesson that you need to learn. Imagine that [they are] an instrument that God is using to teach you a lesson and give you an opportunity to grow spiritually. Your negative response stems from the fact that you are not looking at the situation as a teaching, lesson, challenge, and opportunity to grow."

I know it's hard to think of what we have lost as "an opportunity to grow spiritually." But it actually is. That doesn't mean it isn't painful, because it is. Terribly painful. But I have been frankly amazed at how I have grown through this awful ordeal with our son and his wife. It has made me much more thoughtful and sensitive toward others, and has caused me to reflect on the mystery of life and death in ways I had never done before. And it has made me more accepting of life and its unpredictability than I ever believed I could be.

I remember what Elizabeth Edwards, wife of presidential candidate John Edwards, wrote in her book *Resilience*, the story of how she dealt with the revelation that her husband had been unfaithful to her with a young videographer in his campaign. She said she was despondent at first, and thought her life had fallen apart. But then she pulled herself together and began to work on remaking her existence with the new thing she had learned. Her life would never be the same again, she said; but she would incorporate what had happened and manage to go on in spite of it.

That's what we parents have to do after Humpty has fallen off the wall. Nothing is ever the same again. But we have to pick ourselves up and go on in spite of that. We have to refashion our lives without the son we have lost—and, if there are grandchildren, without them as well.

THE IMPORTANCE OF SPIRITUAL RESOURCES

Spiritual reserves and ways of handling difficulties differ from person to person and religion to religion. Buddhists and Hindus usually absorb suffering by reminding themselves it is only transitory and that they may be more fortunate in the next reincarnation if they bear their misfortunes well in this one. Muslims simply appeal to Allah for justice and the endurance to bear their pain. "Please, our Lord," says the Qur'an, "do not make us carry that for which we lack the strength." Christians, taught to pray and forgive others, submit their needs to God and ask divine forgiveness for their children and themselves.

Whatever one's belief system and religious practice, a rupture with one's son and his family is the time to call on these foundational resources. There are few occasions in life when we need them more. If we are fortunate, they will well up like water from some deep underground spring, bringing hope and healing.

It happened for me while I was writing this book.

One morning my husband I were lying in bed, telling each other our dreams. He said he had a very complicated dream in which he had become pastor of a large congregation, and the first service was adjourned from the sanctuary to a concert hall where I was conducting a symphony I had written. He wanted to listen to the music but kept getting called away for other things and therefore missed the whole concert.

It was interesting that he dreamed about me in a musical setting, as my own dream was also about music. I was in a place where a popular African American minister was conducting a radio show and he insisted that I play something on the piano. I hesitated because I didn't feel that I could add anything to his program, but at last I agreed to play.

Instead of offering something classical, I began to play and sing a chorus I learned in church as a young girl:

Got any rivers you think are uncrossable?
Got any mountains you cannot tunnel through?
God specializes in things that seem impossible.
He knows a thousand ways to make a way for you!

As we talked about our dreams, we realized that they both had to do with the tensions we were feeling from dealing with Richard and Monica. My concert, in my husband's dream, was symbolic of my writing this book. I was doing something each day that he wanted to be there for, but, because he had other obligations to fill, he couldn't fully participate in. The suggestion of my own dream was that I should leave my problem with our son in the hands of God, who knows how to make things work out for the best.

LEARN TO FORGIVE

It is important, in this whole messy business, to forgive our sons for what they have done or failed to do. It isn't easy. We probably feel that they have insulted our love and have betrayed and hurt us immeasurably. But we need to be able to forgive them, if only for our own sakes.

I thought I had forgiven Richard. But after the initial forgiveness I found that there were more levels of feeling to deal with. I assumed, when I first forgave him, that that was all there was to it. But then I reached another level where I discovered I must go through even more anguish. After that one, I reached yet another level and had to contend with more difficulties than before. The levels seemed to go on descending interminably, and getting more and more complicated as they went. But I patiently worked through each one, realizing that I wouldn't have any peace until I reached the absolute inner core where I actually meant it when I said that I forgave him.

Grown children, I have found, are sometimes angry with parents not because we have done anything but because they themselves have failed at something. This could have been true of our son Richard. When he was young, he dreamed he would be a successful artist. He also talked of becoming a millionaire by the time he was thirty.

But two things happened to thwart his dreams.

First, they're not called "starving artists" for nothing. Our son barely earned enough to exist. He worked hard and produced some beautiful paintings, but he learned that unless an artist has earned a reputation, so that his or her paintings are valuable, it is very difficult to sell them.

And second, his first wife became very impatient with their marriage because he didn't make enough to buy her all the luxuries she wanted. She got to the point where she was constantly dropping hints and insults about his inability to sell enough paintings to fulfill her expectations. As she had been the love of his life, her disappointment hurt him very deeply and caused him to regard himself as a failure.

If he was a failure, he had several choices about whom to blame. He could blame himself, and say, "Well, I wasn't as good as I thought I was, or I would have sold a lot of paintings and my wife would not have become unhappy with me." He could blame his wife for not supporting and encouraging him as she should. Or he could blame his parents. His parents, after all, had set him up for failure in this difficult world by pretending (a) it was a kinder place than it was, and (b) he was a better artist than he was.

He possibly concluded that we had not prepared him adequately for life as it is. He felt let down, and we were the evil monsters who had caused it.

That choice, if indeed it was the one he made, was what I needed to forgive him for. I thought he must be undergoing some awful pain and confusion to behave the way he was behaving toward us. My mother's heart went out to him. I couldn't bear my child's enormous suffering. I wanted to take it away from him and make it my own.

The only way I knew to do that was to forgive him.

At our final meeting with him, in that awful encounter in a restaurant, I had to tell him. I knew he wouldn't be able to hear me, but I had to tell him I was sorry for the estrangement and that I forgave him for it.

He said, "Why do you say you're sorry?"

I doubled my right hand, clasped it to my heart, and replied, "Because I'm a Christian."

I don't know what made me say that. I don't normally talk about my religion. I'm a firm believer in practicing my faith without announcing it. But that day in the restaurant there wasn't any other reason I could think of for what I had said. If I had been a Buddhist, I might have said, "Because I am a Buddhist." If I had been a Muslim, I might have said, "Because I am a Muslim." But in this case I said what I said because love and forgiveness are the very heart and core of what I believe as a Christian, and I was acting out of the absolute center of who I am.

I wanted to be whole again—desperately needed to be— and I didn't think I could be until I had forgiven my son.

FIND ANOTHER FOCUS

As hard as I fought against it, I was beginning to obsess over what had happened in our family. Morning, noon, and night, that image of Humpty-Dumpty preyed on my mind. It was all I could think about. I thought about it when I was talking, when I was eating, when I watched TV, when I tried to read, when I was riding in the car, when I did housework. I couldn't stop dwelling on it.

My husband and I went to England and France for a month. He thought we'd both feel better just getting away from home. But wherever we went, what had happened went with us. We had lived in Paris in 1967-1968 when Richard was a small boy. Everywhere we looked we saw his face. The family had lived in England in 1977-1978, and we remembered all the places where we had gone with Richard and how much fun we had had together.

Later that same summer, we attended the Shaw Festival at Niagara-on-the-Lake, Ontario, and saw eight plays in four days. They were all great plays beautifully produced. But just when I would catch myself enjoying them the most, something in my head clicked and I began hearing those old tapes about Richard and our family.

I normally love to read, and go through two or three books a week. But during this period of obsession with Richard and what had happened I found myself rereading a paragraph for the fifth or sixth time without really understanding it. Then I would lay my book aside and my mind would churn over all the facts again, trying to make sense of the awful estrangement we were experiencing.

It was as if I was walking through an extraordinarily thick fog and the only things I could make out in it were the figures of my son and his family.

My husband is retired, though he still goes faithfully to his study each day. We had a lot of time to brood on Richard and this terrible impasse we had come to with him. We always dreamed that the focus of our elder years would be on our children and grandchildren. But now we were faced by a giant void where Richard and his family had been. It was as if some enormous psychic explosion had removed them and we didn't know what to do with the rest of our lives.

In Rosamunde Pilcher's *September* (I know I mentioned Pilcher before; she's a favorite), a character named Violet is beginning to notice her age and contemplate it. Pilcher says: "The worst part of growing old, Violet decided, was that happiness, at the most inappropriate times, eluded one. She should feel happy now, but did not."

That's how it was with us. We should have felt happy, but we didn't. We couldn't. Everything we had hoped for and counted on had fallen through. To us personally, it was a disaster of near cosmic proportions!

We both knew we had to start reinventing our lives. We had to contemplate an existence that didn't include our son and his family. We began looking for property in other states, where we would no longer be near Richard and his children. My husband began new writing projects.

I started this book.

We haven't yet laid the ghost of what has happened to us. We may never, entirely.

But we are working on it. It's all we can do!

FRIENDS WHO STARTED OVER

One day I stopped by to help our friends Emmet and Trish pack for a move. Trish was slowly packing up mementoes she and Emmet had collected on their trips around the world. Fondly, she recalled the place of each one's origin. She said she could still smell the distinctive odor of each city or country represented by the keepsakes. Normally she acted swiftly and efficiently. But now she was moving slowly, thoughtfully, trying to recapture her whole life in the little things she was wrapping and packing.

Trish and Emmet had moved to our area a couple of years ago to be near their only son, Chad, his wife Teresa, and a new grandson named Carson. They had come with high hopes for a good life together, but those hopes soon began to evaporate. Teresa was very jealous of Chad's time and attention, and appeared to resent her in-laws' presence. She particularly resented their affection for little Carson.

"It's almost as if she lays her body down at the door," said Trish, "and dares us to enter his room."

As Teresa's behavior became more and more overtly hostile, Trish and Emmet decided to bow out of their children's lives and move to Florida. They considered moving back to their home state of Oklahoma, but decided instead to cast their lot with all the other people who had moved to the Sunshine State in search of peace and happiness in their later years.

"As difficult as it is to leave our son and grandson," Trish told me, "we have to learn to live without them. I keep telling myself we'll make new friends, walk the beach at sunrise and sunset, eat our fill of seafood, find new outlets for shopping, and try to reorient our lives. We have to. We don't have any other options."

Their spirits weren't soaring as they packed for this move, but Trish and Emmet were probably doing the wise thing. If they stayed where they were, they would continue to run into high levels of hostility from Teresa that might eventually poison their relationship with Chad. They didn't want to put pressure on Chad by staying, either. So moving away seemed the best thing to do. At least it bore the positive implication that they could find a good life without their son and his family.

———◦———

There are a lot of needy people in the world. One thing we can all do when our sons and their wives shut us out of their families is to adopt some of those persons and concentrate on them and what we can do for them instead of merely nursing our own wounds all the time.

There are many things we can do to help. We can get involved as teachers' helpers, deliver Meals on Wheels, work for Habitat for Humanity, read to children at the public library, invite young couples into our homes for dinner, start programs in our churches or synagogues for helping prisoners and their families, and a host of other things. In fact, the opportunities to become involved with others and their needs is limited only by the size of our imagination.

The first Christmas we spent without our son and his family, we had a closetful of gifts we had purchased during the year for our grandchildren. One mechanical toy we bought in Canada made crazy, erratic movements and had a lot of lights, bells, and whistles. We knew it would be a big hit with our lively, expressive granddaughter Abigail, as it was just the sort of thing children delight in.

We wrapped these gifts, hoping against hope that our son and his wife would relent at the last minute and bring the children to see us. We even considered taking the presents to their house, but decided in the end that such an action would be construed as an unwelcome invasion of their space. So we hoped they would come to us.

On Christmas Day, when we had had no contact with our son and his family, we bundled up all the presents and took them to a young family we knew in a nearby neighborhood who had told us a week or two earlier that they were taking bankruptcy and letting the bank assume ownership of their home. We knew the parents would buy a few things for their three little children, but realized they couldn't do as much as they liked because of the lean time they were going through. We had a pang in our hearts that it wasn't our own grandchildren we were taking the presents to, but what we were doing was better than sitting at home and doing nothing.

The hardest present for me to give away to somebody else's children was an unusual jewelry box we had gotten for Abigail. It was made like a miniature house and was enchantingly decorated with little rose-covered trellises. The roof was hinged, and when it was opened back there was space for all sorts of jewelry. If a drawer was pulled out, a music box played. I had filled the toy house with a lot of plastic and wooden jewelry so that Abigail could play dress-up like her mommy. It hurt me not to be able to see Abigail open this present. But it was at least a modest consolation to know that another three-year-old would enjoy playing with it.

In addition to the presents for the children, we took a lovely Christmas card for the parents with a note of encouragement and five one-hundred-dollar bills in it. We knew it was only a pittance compared with their enormous needs at the time, but at least it would say to them that we cared about their pain.

A few days after Christmas, the entire family came by our house with a thank-you note and a loaf of delicious banana bread the young mother had made. It warmed our hearts, and helped us to realize that even the darkest times in our lives can be made lighter by reaching out to others who're in need.

———◇———

Following the births of our grandchildren, our house became a virtual picture gallery. I sometimes joked that my husband and I were the caretakers of a shrine to our grandkids. Every day, I reveled in going from room to room and being greeted in each place by their smiling faces.

But after we became estranged from our son and his wife, I became choked up at seeing the same pictures that had earlier brought me so much joy. So I decided it was time to pack most of them away. I simply couldn't bear looking at them all the time. I tucked them into various empty drawers and stowed the children's toys and books in the basement.

Our basement was already finished when we moved into the house. In the main room on that floor, we had made a huge picture gallery of photographs of our two sons as they were growing up. Now, looking at those pictures made me very sad, especially when I stared at the ones of the blond-headed little fellow who had grown up and told us he hated us and never wanted to see us again. So one day I took down the entire display, packed up the photos, patched up the holes where the nails had been, and repainted the wall. I felt a certain remorse in doing it, but I knew it needed to be done. I would feel better if I didn't have to look at those images of our son any more.

One of the things Rabbi Harold Kushner said in his famous book, *When Bad Things Happen to Good People*, is that people who have been deeply hurt by something tend to compound the damage by hurting themselves a second time. They do this by fastening on the very sources of their rejection, bereavement, injury, or bad luck as if they themselves were to blame for it. They torture themselves by reliving the past or making shrines out of the very persons and circumstances that inflicted the hurt in the first place. The sooner we can write *finis* to the past and move on, the better.

As our friend Phyllis Stump says in her poem "Loss," in *Walking the Gunnysack Trail,*

> Fly away,
> Don't look back
> On what will never be.

It may not be what we planned but there is life after what our children have done to us.

GETTING ON WITH IT

When we get older we have a tendency to think of ourselves as being spent, used up, exhausted. But we often forget what remarkable things many older people have done, some of them doubtless after great disappointments with family members.

Grandma Moses began her meteoric career as an artist at the ripe age of 70.

Michaelangelo finished painting his famous fresco on the ceiling of the Sistine Chapel at the Vatican when he was 79.

Helen Thomas, the well known reporter who began covering the White House in 1961, is now in her 80s, regularly attends White House news conferences, and channels her energies into two weekly editorials for the Hearst Newspaper Corporation.

Our good friend Chester Burger was 86 when he produced a best-selling book called *Unexpected New York*, for which he took his own brilliant photographs. Now almost 90, he has continued to lead an active life, flying all over the U.S. as a public relations consultant for U.S. military forces.

Martha Graham danced professionally until she was 76 and then worked as a choreographer into her 90s.

Architect Frank Lloyd Wright worked on the Guggenheim Museum until he was well into his 90s.

Dr. Ray Crist, the famous environmentalist, who is now more than 100 years old, still goes each day to his laboratory in Pennsylvania's Messiah College, where he continues to solve vexing ecological problems.

We shouldn't ever think or feel that getting older and losing a son means the end of the road. There is still time to go out and make another life or learn to enjoy a world at which we barely looked before. We can buy the boat or RV we always wanted to buy, or visit the country we dreamed of visiting. We can learn yoga, take up watercoloring, or even learn to ski.

There was a recent news story about an 87-year-old woman who parachuted out of an airplane. She bounced a couple of times as she landed, but got up as spry as a youngster. Asked what she was feeling, she said, "Two things. First, it was wonderful! Second, I need to find my teeth!"

What's the famous bumper-sticker slogan, "We're spending our children's inheritance"?

That's the spirit! Why not?!

REACH OUT TO OTHERS

Remember, we aren't the only parents who have had a problem with an disrespectful son and a mean-spirited daughter-in-law. Our name is Legion. Almost every day I read or hear about someone who is part of our growing fellowship.

That's why I decided to write this book. I wanted to tell some of their stories so they would be available to readers who thought they were the only ones who had traveled this lonesome road.

If I had been more of an organizer, I would have posted a notice on community bulletin boards inviting grieving parents to come and talk about their problems, the way AA members get together, or relatives of Alzheimer's patients. Those who have a gift for starting new organizations should do this. There are few things more therapeutic for most people than sitting around a room with others who have similar stories and sharing their experiences.

It has done me a world of good to hear the stories I've shared in this book. I've learned that there is a virtual epidemic of sons turning on their parents these days and creating rifts in families that once considered themselves rock solid and impregnable to division. It has helped me to realize that what happened in our family wasn't my fault and that I didn't necessarily do something in raising my son that made him dislike me and turn against me as an adult.

I have been reminded again and again of how common our experiences are, and how they tend to be repeated from generation to generation. It's easy to get to thinking we are unique, that no one else has encountered grief and suffering the way we have, and that we are therefore in a class by ourselves. We aren't. We soon learn, when we look around, that we're all in this together, and that whatever happens to us has happened to others in deuces and treys. I have often cried over the stories of some of the parents I've talked with, and wondered how they've managed to hold on to their sanity. Some of them have been more deeply insulted, neglected, and hurt than I have.

What happens as we reach out to others can be a kind of spiritual experience, for it tends to deepen our respect for humanity and the shocks and injuries it manages to withstand. It makes us think about parents with all kinds of problems all over the world, including those who can't feed their starving children in Darfur or shelter their endangered offspring in Afghanistan or heal their suffering little ones in the slums of Calcutta.

In the face of all the suffering, we can only bow our heads in shame for having focused so much on our own miseries and ask whatever Higher Power we believe in to help those who are less fortunate than we are. Then we can go out and put our arms around some of those people and attempt to share the enormous burdens they are carrying.

That's what I've hoped to do in this book. I've wanted to say to you what I always said to the son who doesn't speak to us any more: "I love you and my arms are around you!"

MEMORIES AND DREAMS

Ah, but we die to each other daily.
What we know of other people
Is only our memory of the moments
During which we knew them.

— T. S. Eliot, *The Cocktail Party*

I T HAS NOW BEEN DEMONSTRATED BY scientists that we
can actually alter our memories of things that happened. I'm
not clever enough to understand how it works, but it has to do
with the complicated way in which neurons in the brain con-
tinually massage the memories being trundled through them.
When memories are recalled, they come back in a muddled
state. If they are very unpleasant—say recollections of being
beaten or mistreated in childhood—our chemical reaction is

such that we actually wish to alter them, and that does something to the brain to edit and make them more palatable. When they are reshelved in their storage places, they have been subtly but surely altered, and the next time they are called forth, it will be the revised versions that we get, not the originals.

I'm sure that in time those of us who have had horrible experiences with our sons and their wives may make some minor inroads on the way we remember them, so that we can tolerate them more than we do now. But for now it is very difficult to elude the hurt we feel at being betrayed by a member of our inner family. Those memories remain extremely vivid and painful.

I recently went through a timeline of the things that happened between Richard and Monica and my husband and me. It's really my husband's timeline—he's the diarist in the family—but everything he had written down evoked keen recollections of the distress we suffered.

It was all there: how Monica charmed us at first; the way she began to maneuver Richard out of our family and into hers, playing him like a game fish she had caught; the day I went with her and her mother to the fitting of her wedding dress and they instructed me that I wasn't to buy a dress for myself without first checking with them; the Easter dinner we didn't have because Monica decided to have a brunch with her brother and his partner and not come to our house until late afternoon; the quibbling over where their rehearsal dinner would be and how many people they could invite; their withdrawal of the invitation for Richard's dad to perform the wedding ceremony; their leaving our names off their wedding invitations, as if Richard were an orphan; our decision not to attend the wedding because we felt systematically shut out of everything; our ceremony of burying their photograph in the woods on Mackinac Island the day of the wedding, and our dinner that evening where we toasted their happiness; their visit to my husband in a Detroit hospital when he almost died; our extremely tentative reconciliation for a couple of years; Monica's growing displeasure with us as we bonded with our granddaughter Abigail, and her and Richard's puzzling dismissal of us when the second granddaughter was born; the quiet showdown my husband arranged in our den after we gave a birthday lunch for Richard; the long period when they wouldn't answer our phone calls or e-mails; Richard's grudging appearance at the restaurant the day he told us he hated us and never wanted to see us again; and the long, unbroken silence ever since.

I ran across references to dreams we had both had.

One of my husband's occurred the night after we had visited Richard and Monica in her condo before they married and she had gotten all over Richard for shutting up her dog because he was bothering us as we tried to talk. John dreamed he was in a restaurant in Paris, where we once lived, and needed to go to the bathroom. A waiter showed him where the men's room was. After he had gone, he found there was no paper, so he called the waiter back. The waiter handed him some sheets of paper, but when he examined them he found that there was dried excrement on them. Outside, he realized in disgust that he had failed to wash his hands. Then he noticed that the streets were running with water. On closer examination, he saw that it wasn't water but sewage. He saw a man fall face down into it.

His own note on the dream suggested that it was related to having been in Monica's condo and coming away feeling dirty and contaminated.

My dream, a couple of weeks after my husband's, was that I was with two other people and we were looking at our photographs of Richard and Monica and weeping over them as if they were dead.

I cannot believe now how prescient that dream was! They are, in effect, dead to us, and we are trying to move on. We are looking for a place to move, in order to get away from the area where Richard and Monica and their precious children live.

We are also making other plans—visits to countries we've never seen, learning languages we can't speak, and generally getting on with our lives. We don't want to be entombed with a son we once knew but who has chosen to forget us or with the memories of grandbabies we'll probably never see again.

We take heart from a minister friend who several years ago lost one of his sons in a terrible accident. Press on, he advised us, for with the passing of time new growth occurs and life becomes beautiful and peaceful again.

"I realize I had more closure than you will have with your son," he said. "But God will provide your own kind of closure as the years go by."

It's true. I can feel it already.

Still, the dreams come. One night recently my husband shook me and said I was sobbing uncontrollably in my sleep. He took me in his arms and tried to comfort me as I told him what I had been dreaming.

I dreamed that he and I went into a restaurant for dinner. We spotted our son Richard sitting at a table with a woman we didn't recognize. We went over to speak to him, but he was so withdrawn and rude that it made me cry.

His dinner companion, a woman I'd never seen, stood up and put her arms around me. "He doesn't know what he is saying," she whispered. "His wife threw him out and he can't visit his own children."

She went on to explain that she was a psychiatric nurse and our son was in therapy with the doctor for whom she worked.

My heart bled for our son. He was emaciated. His eyes were sunk deep into his head and had black circles under them. His expression was the saddest I had ever seen. But in all his agony, he let me know he didn't want my assistance in any way.

I kept thinking, "What is wrong with him? Can't he understand that I only want to hug him and let him know I'm here if he needs me?"

My mother's heart won't let him go completely. He'll always have a place there, even though he has repeatedly rejected it. And because of that I'll probably always have dreams like this one in which I try to reach out and comfort him.

In a way, that's as it should be. If I didn't love him, none of what has happened would have mattered anyway.

When we lived in New York, three years after our final break with Richard and Monica—my husband was executive minister and theologian for famous Marble Collegiate Church—I wrote Monica a letter telling her where we were. I told her there wasn't a day that went by when I didn't think about them, and that I often stopped in St. Patrick's Cathedral, where I lit candles for each of them and the children and prayed for them. As she was Roman Catholic, I thought she might appreciate this gesture.

"I always say the same prayer," I wrote, "for God to keep you safe and happy. It makes my day lighter when I know those candles will burn long after I have left the church. It is as if there will be a protective cloak of love around you."

I told her I wished we could resolve the problems "keeping us from being the loving family we used to be." I didn't want to infringe on their space, I said. But it would be nice if we could see each other every few weeks, at least. Life is "too short and precious" to allow whatever differences she and Richard felt existed between us to keep us apart forever.

But Monica didn't answer.

Wondering if perhaps she didn't get the letter—surely they hadn't moved?—I sent a copy of the letter to Richard's school and asked him to give it to her.

Again there was no answer.

Several months later, I tried to call them. Our son Eric was having serious surgery and I wanted them to know and get in touch with him.

They didn't answer, but I left a message.

Twice.

Again, no response.

So that's where it is with us. One day we will find another place and move on. So will Eric and his wife.

It's a sad business for those of us who have always loved our families.

But what can you do?

As novelist Ernest Hemingway once said, you play the cards you're dealt. It's the only hand you have.

CPSIA information can be obtained at www.ICGtesting.com
Printed in the USA
BVOW05s2233201014

371639BV00001B/54/P